BOOK OF CHANGES

AN INTERPRETATION
for the MODERN AGE

易话人生

TEXT BY
CHAN CHIU MING

CALLIGRAPHY BY
XU QINGHUA

ASIAPAC. SINGAPORE

Publisher
ASIAPAC BOOKS PTE LTD
629 Aljunied Road
#04-06 Cititech Industrial Building
Singapore 389838
Tel: (65) 7453868
Fax: (65) 7453822
Email apacbks@singnet.com.sg

Visit us at our Internet home page
http://www.span.com.au/asiapac.htm

First published January 1997

©1997 ASIAPAC BOOKS, SINGAPORE
ISBN 981-3068-29-9

Cover design by Marked Point Design
Body text in Garamond 11pt
Printed in Singapore by Kin Keong Printing Co Pte Ltd

Publisher's Note

Book of Changes: An Interpretation for the Modern Age is unique in that it combines the writing of Chinese scholar Chan Chiu Ming and the calligraphy of Chinese artist Xu Qinghua, together with the classic text of the *Book of Changes*.

Both works featured are attested to be in a class of their own. Firstly, the author has demonstrated a precise understanding of the words, images and styles of the original, having examined the works of ancient and modern Chinese authorities. Secondly, the calligrapher has elegantly expressed in the four major forms of the Chinese script the most crucial words in the "Ten Wings" classic text, traditionally ascribed to Confucius. This edition will certainly prove to deepen your knowledge of the ancient classic and enhance your application of this Chinese art of divination.

We would like to thank Chan Chiu Ming and Xu Qinghua for the making of this unprecedented volume, and to Zheng Zhong for the foreword. Our thanks, too, to the production team for putting in their best efforts to make this publication possible.

About the Author

Dr Chan Chiu Ming obtained his BA (Hons) in Chinese and Translation from the University of Hong Kong and his MA and PhD from the University of Wisconsin-Madison. An expert in Chinese literature and culture, he is well-versed in the classics, including the *Book of Changes*. He has taught courses on Chinese Literature, Philosophical Taoism and Chinese Culture at the University of Wisconsin. An experienced translator, he took part in the translation of the *Shiji*, published by the Indiana University in 1995. Presently, he lectures in the Division of Chinese Language and Culture in the Nanyang Technological University, Singapore.

About the Calligrapher

Styled Liaoyi and alias Yizhai, Xu Qinghua was born in Shanghai. He is a teaching staff of the Arts Research Branch of the Jiaotong University, Shanghai and is concurrently Associate Professor of the Hainan Vocational University.

An accomplished calligrapher, he is a member of the famous Xiying Calligraphy Society, and the Xiling Society of the Seal Engraving Art. He has taken part in various national exhibitions, including the distinguished "Exhibition of Select Works of One Hundred Contemporary Chinese Calligraphers" and the "Biennial International Exhibition of Modern Calligraphy, 96".

His biography is also included in over twenty dictionaries of calligraphy and arts, such as *Biographies of Contemporary Writers and Artists*; *Chinese Artists*; and *Selected Works of Modern Calligraphers*.

Foreword

The *Book of Changes* has since ancient times been regarded as the first among the six classics and is one of the *Three Classics of Profound Mystery* (i.e. *Laozi, Zhuangzi* and *Book of Changes*).

The earliest extant handwritten copies of the *Book of Changes* are found among the Mawangdui and Dunhuang manuscripts. They were written on bamboo slips. The Ming dynasty (1368-1644) scholar Wang Yangming (1472-1529) and artist Huang Daozhou (1585-1646) had handwritten phrases and words abstracted from the *Book of Changes*.

Compared to Wang Yangming and Huang Daozhou's works, the words and phrases brushed by Mr Xu Qinghua is more systematic. Totalling 404 characters, they are the most essential words abstracted from the *xiang* parts of all sixty-four hexagrams and appear in all four major forms of the Chinese script. I call this ingenious undertaking the "New Brush-copying of the Classics".

Mr Xu Qinghua, still in his prime, has immersed deeply in the traditional art and mastered various styles of calligraphy. His calligraphy exhibits a sense of serenity and a distinctive style of his own. He manifests a flexibility within the best tradition. In short, he has resisted the trend of the strange and baroque of many contemporary calligraphers, and has cultivated a fresh and natural grace. Such a graceful style is probably what he also strives for in his calligraphy.

Zheng Zhong
October 1996, China

Contents

III   APPENDICES

Introduction

I) The Three Layers of the *Book of Changes*

Referred to by traditional Chinese scholars as *the first* among the classics, the *Book of Changes* is one of the most important books for every student of Chinese culture. For the last two thousand years, people have been consulting it for guidance in major decisions. Yet the *I Ching,* or *Yijing* as we call the book in Chinese, actually comprises three layers.

The first layer consists of the **eight trigrams**, which Chinese tradition ascribes to the legendary sage emperor Fu Xi (traditionally dated around 2852 B.C.). Though this theory cannot be substantiated, the antiquity of the *Book of Changes* it implies is generally recognized. The second layer comprises the **sixty-four hexagrams** and the "Judgement" as well as the "texts" expounding the significance of the lines of the hexagrams. According to Chinese tradition, it was King Wen of the Zhou dynasty (fl. 1080 B.C.) who doubled the trigrams and invented the sixty-four hexagrams. He was also believed to be the author of the brief "judgements" of the hexagrams. His son, the Duke of Zhou (fl. 1066 B.C.), later wrote the "texts" which expounded the significance of the individual lines. Though one may hesitate to ascribe the layer actually to the two sages, it is generally agreed that the hexagrams and the "texts" were a product of the early Zhou dynasty. In most versions of the *Book of Changes* as we have it now, there are also commentaries on the hexagrams and the "texts" of the lines. Called the **"Ten Wings"**, these were traditionally ascribed to Confucius. A number of scholars challenge this view and suggest that the "Ten Wings" are of a much later date. Recently, Liao Mingchun has argued convincingly that the "Ten Wings" were actually written by Confucius and his disciples.[1]

Students of Confucianism would find this third layer of immense significance. Yet the Confucian overtone of this layer deviates from the nature of the first two layers. To the modern reader who wants to have some guidance and advice, but not heavy moral precepts, the first and second layers are perhaps more relevant. Together, these two layers are sometimes referred to as the *gujing*, or *Ancient Canon*. One may say that this is the original *Book of Changes*. The main body of this Translation is that of the original one. However, to give the reader a glimpse of the Confucian view, the *xiang*, or the Confucian commentaries on the significance of the hexagrams as a whole, are also translated (though those on the "texts" of the lines are omitted). They are set on separate pages below the beautiful calligraphies, which actually comprise key words abstracted from the *xiang*.

II) Modern Significance of the *Book of Changes*

A century ago, the great sinologist James Legge reported that Chinese scholars of his time were fond of saying that "all the truths of electricity, light, heat, and other branches of 'European' physics are in the eight trigrams". He admonished that unless the Chinese "drop their hallucination about the *Yi* as containing all things", "it will prove a stumbling block to them"[2]. The awesome Joseph Needham lent his authority to Legge's theory.[3] However, despite what Legge and Needham say, many modern scholars have shown that the *Book of Changes* is still relevant to modern science. *Yijing* symbology has been shown to be a kind of "biochemical dictionary"[4]. Similarities have been found between the *Yijing* concepts and quantum theory.[5] Some scholars even try to draw inspiration from the *Book of Changes* in their studies of DNA structures.[6] Attempts have also been made to apply the *Yijing* principles in communication studies.[7] Given the fact that many modern scientists continue to draw inspirations from the *Book of Changes*, it is hard to dismiss the insights that the *Book of Changes* offers as mere coincidence, as Needham seems to have suggested in the case of the similarity of the *Yijing* structure as expounded by Shao Yong (A.D.1011-1077) and the binary theory of Leibniz.[8]

The validity of the *Book of Changes* in modern science is a matter for debate for students of science. In the debate, many scholars seem to have failed to distinguish the *Book of Changes* itself from the cosmogony and systems of thought derived from it. The question, however, that a layman may want to ask is: In what ways are the *Book of Changes* relevant in our daily life? This leads us to another question: How does the *Book of Changes* "divine"?

III) How the *Book of Changes* "Divines"

As scholars generally agree, the original *Book of Changes* is a book of divination. Fung Yu-lan, an authority of Chinese philosophy, proposes that the word "yi" in *Yijing* means "easy" and the *Book of Changes* is in fact a "Book of Divination made easy"[9].

Given this nature of the book, many a modern man may dismiss it as a book of superstition. Yet for centuries, people have been consulting it for guidance, and in many cases the prognostications it makes are recorded to be correct. Even modern scholars are amazed by the accuracy of its predictions. The renowned psychiatrist Carl J. Jung has attested that the oracles he got concerning whether he was qualified to write the foreword to Wilhelm's translation of the *Book of Changes* all turned out to be relevant and are sound advices. He believes that the accuracy of the *Book of Changes* can be explained by the principle of "synchronicity", which "takes the coincidence of events in space and time as meaning something more than chance, namely, a peculiar interdependence of objective events among themselves as well as with the subjective (psychic) states of the observer or observers."[10]

A.C. Graham, a leading world authority on Chinese thought and grammar, echoes Jung on the validity of the *Book of Changes* as a guide for decision-making. He observes that the *Book of Changes* is more successful than most divination systems in guiding people to reach appropriate decisions "in situations with too many unknown factors."[11] However, rather than the a-causal principle of synchronicity, he believes that the *Book of Changes* functions because it "serves to break down preconceptions by forcing the diviner to correlate his situation with a chance sequence of six prognostications." And since the hexagrams "open up an indefinite range of patterns for correlation, in the calm of withdrawal into sacred space and time, the effect is to free the mind to take account of all information whether or not it conflicts with preconceptions, awaken it to unnoticed similarities and connexions." [12] The word "sacred" must be emphasized here, for without a true reverence to the *Yijing* or, if one does not believe in the existence of a divine will, the divine spirit that speaks through it, one will not be able to actually free his thought from preconceptions. Without the reverence, one may draw one hexagram, and then ask for another, and thus end up coming back to one's own preconceptions.

For the more religious-minded, the *Book of Changes* functions in a different dimension. John Blofeld has compared what Graham describes as the "withdrawal into sacred space and time" to *zen* (or in Chinese, *chan*) meditation.[13] For a Taoist, the *Yijing* works by guiding one to see his own position and role in the natural flow of the current of Time and events. One who believes in the existence of the Divine may read the hexagrams as the symbols through which the Divine indicates His advice and the "texts" as His cryptic words meaningful only to those who have faith.

All the above theories, secular or otherwise, suggest that the *Book of Changes* functions well as a repertoire of sound advice and guidance. In whatever theory, "reverence" is the key word to reemphasize.

IV) Key Concepts and Structure of the *Book of Changes*

It is pointed out above that Confucius and his disciples authored the "Ten Wings", which are commentaries on the *Book of Changes*. That the sage, who did not speak of the supernatural things,[14] would write commentaries on a book of divination may sound strange. Citing a Mawang Dui manuscript, Liao Mingchun observes that Confucius was interested in the book not as a manual of divination, but as a work that contains the teachings of the ancient sages.[15] Scholars after Confucius also endeavoured to find out from the *Book of Changes* important philosophical insights. A notable figure was Wang Bi (A.D. 226-249). Summarized below are the key concepts essential for an understanding of the philosophy of the *Yijing*.

1) *Yin* and *Yang*

Yin and *Yang* are conceived to be the two forces that make up all things in the universe. *Yin* is represented by a divided line (- -) while *yang* by an undivided line (—). *Yin* is often associated with the feminine, the moon, darkness, and such qualities as submissiveness, the yielding and the receptive. *Yang* represents the masculine, the sun, brightness and such qualities as assertiveness, aggressiveness and the creative. Though scholars since the Han dynasty often regarded *yang* as superior and *yin* as inferior, in the *Book of Changes* itself the two are complementary to each other. Whether a *yin* or a *yang* line indicates good fortune or misfortune depends not on its own quality alone, but also on the Time and the Position it occupies. In modern terms, one may say that this implies that whether one will meet with success or failure depends not only on one's disposition or talent, but on the Time and the Position one is in. The man of wisdom will be contented with a Position that suits his disposition or ability at the Time given.

When applied to social situations, *yin* and *yang* are not constant. At any given Time, one is *yin* relative to his superior, but is *yang* to his subordinates. At a different Time, he may have ascended to a higher Position than his former superior and will become *yang* in relation to the same person. The relativity of the concepts of *yin* and *yang* embodies the concept of change.

Generally speaking, a hexagram portends of great fortune if there is harmony of the *yin* and *yang*, the feminine and the masculine, and the submissive and the aggressive.

2) Trigrams and Hexagrams

Three lines make up one trigram. All together there are eight trigrams. Each trigram symbolizes different phenomena and qualities. The following is a summary of the most important symbolic significance of the eight trigrams:

☰	Qian	Heaven, the Assertive, ruler, father, dragon, horse, Northwest,
☷	Kun	Earth, Inner Strength, the Yielding, subjects, mother, mare, ox, Southwest
☳	Zhen	Thunder, Shock, young men, eldest son, galloping horse, flying dragon, East
☵	Kan	Water/clouds, Abyss, thieves, second son, pig, North
☶	Gen	Mountain, Steadiness, gatekeepers, youngest son, dog, rat, Northeast
☴	Xun	Wind/wood, the Yielding, merchants, eldest daughter, hen, Southeast
☲	Li	Fire, Fiery Temper, sun, masculine women, second daughter, pheasant, toad, tortoise, South
☱	Dui	Swamp, the Pleasing, enchantresses, youngest daughter, concubine, sheep, West

Each hexagram consists of two trigrams—a lower and an

upper one. As each trigram can be regarded as a symbol, one may also say that each hexagram comprises two symbols. The combined significance of the symbols gives the hexagram its symbolic meaning. The lower trigram is also called the inner trigram while the upper one the outer trigram. The different names of the pairs indicate different significance one associates with the trigrams. The terms "upper" and "lower" indicate the status, while the terms "outer" and "inner" indicate the controllability of the factors. The outer trigram represents the factors that are more or less external, and often beyond one's control. The inner trigram symbolizes the factors which are internal, referring often to such factors as one's attitude, disposition and efforts. In this Translation, the terms "outer" and "inner" are used.

3) *Shi*—Time, Opportune Time and Timing

In Wang Bi's words, each hexagram indicates a *shi*,[16] which can be translated as Time or Opportune Time, and can be understood as the current or the trend of the time, the possible development of events, and the overall situation. Hexagram 1, for example, indicates it is a Time for the Assertive; and Hexagram 4 shows that it is the Time to deal with the Undisciplined.

Yet this is only one aspect of the concept of *shi*. The six lines, or *yao*, make up another aspect. They indicate, to cite Wang Bi again, *shi shi zhi bian zhe*, "the ways in which one changes [his position or strategy] in response to the Time."[17] This, in our terms, is the concept of Timing. In the Time for the Assertive, it is theoretically auspicious for a man to assert himself. Yet besides the Time itself, another factor decides the actual consequence—one's Position at a particular point of time. One's Position is to be a factor considered in the Timing of one's moves.

4) *Wei*—Auspicious Position, Hierarchical Position, and
  Complementary Position

8

Each hexagram comprises six lines. A line may be of the *yang* or the *yin*. The *yin* and *yang* of lines are shown in the forms of the hexagrams. Yet each line occupies a Position, and each Position has its own *yin* or *yang* quality. These qualities of the positions are not shown in the forms of the hexagrams.

The first, third and fifth positions are those of the *yang*, while the second, fourth and sixth positions those of *yin*. If a *yang* line occupies a *yang* position, it is said to be "in the appropriate position". Generally speaking, a line in the appropriate position is an auspicious portent and one may thus call this position the auspicious position.

Besides the *yin* or *yang* quality, each Position also represents the diviner's status in a hierarchy. To the ancient Chinese, the first position (from bottom up) indicates that one has just joined the government and has not gained any recognition. The second position is that of someone who has gained some recognition but has not acquired any fame or power. The third position is for someone who has climbed up the social ladder, though not very powerful yet. The fourth position is the position of a high official close to the ruler. The fifth position is that of the sovereign. The sixth position belongs to those who have retired or should retire. In modern terms, one may argue the six lines correspond to the following positions of (a) the junior officers or workers, (b) the group leaders or foremen, (c) the section heads, (d) department heads or managers, (e) managing director, and (f) members of the board of directors who do not take part in the daily operation of the company.

This aspect of "Hierarchical Position" is important. Though a man of *yang* quality occupies a *yang* position, which is said to be "appropriate", he may still incur disaster if he forgets about his actual position in the hierarchy. Thus in line 1 of Hexagram 1, the divination is that of "A dragon in retreat; don't assert yourself yet." Someone in such a low position, auspicious though it may be, will bring disaster upon himself if he asserts himself. In this case, the concepts of Time and Timing are also involved: though the Time is favourable, bad Timing (i.e. asserting oneself too early) will result in misfortune.

Another vital concept is that of Corresponding Position. Positions 1 & 4, 2 & 5 and 3 & 6 are said to be corresponding to each other. In other words, each line in the lower or inner trigram corresponds with a line in the upper or outer trigram. Ideally, such a pair should comprise one *yin* and one *yang* line. In social terms, someone in a lower position will need the help of someone from above. Yet a person in the higher position must also have the support from the lower. Yet Position 1 corresponds with Position 4 but not with Positions 5 or 6. This is to say that each Position has its own partner. A man of wisdom will first identify his true partner and associate with the corresponding one only. Therefore, though one may want to seek support from above, not everyone at the top will respond. One has to find out who is in a Position that corresponds to one's own.

5) Changes

Traditional scholars attribute three meanings to the word *Yi*: easy; changes; and unchanging. According to this theory, the *Book of Changes* is called the *Yi* because: (a) by following the principles of the *Book of Changes*, one's mind will always be at *ease*; (b) the book has captured all the principles of change behind all the myriad things; and (c) it has captured the unchanging principles, such as the relative positions of Heaven and Earth, and that of the ruler and subjects. A wise man is one who can differentiate the unchanging from the changing, resigning to the former while working on the latter. He is also able to distinguish the factors which are "unchanging" for the Time being from the factors which are unchanging all the times.

The concept of the "unchanging" is best indicated by the

constant nature of the "appropriate positions" and the hierarchy that the positions represent. To the modern reader, the concept of "change" is perhaps more important. As pointed out above, each of the hexagrams symbolizes a certain Time, a certain situation. Yet if only one of the lines changes from *yin* to *yang* or from *yang* to *yin*, we will have another hexagram. Therefore, each of the hexagrams has the potential to become all the other sixty-three hexagrams. The sixty-four hexagrams as a whole represents a cycle of changes, and each of the hexagrams is only a process in the whole cycle. Therefore, the Time or general situation represented by a hexagram is also fluid, though "stable" when compared to the lines.

As explained above, each line is indicative of the *yin* or the *yang*, and each line occupies a Position, which in turn has its own *yin* or *yang* value. Each Position also corresponds to another Position. Therefore, one may say that each of the six lines represents a different condition which accounts for the fortune or misfortune of the diviner in a certain given situation. In our Translation, the lines are therefore listed as the "Conditions". As the conditions have changed, one's behaviour should also be modified, even if the general situation remains the same. In Hexagram 60 we find a classic example of this concept of change. The texts of line 1 reads "Do not venture out of the door. Then there will be no harm." Yet when we come to line 2, the admonishment one gets is "If you do not venture out of the gate, there will be danger." The Time still calls for "Self-restraint", yet a change in the conditions requires a change in strategy.

V) Method of "Divination"

Before describing any method of divination, a question needs to be answered: Why does one have to employ a particular kind of "method"? To one who is not religious-minded, though he may accept Jung or Graham's theories, the question is perhaps more pertinent. I would suggest this answer: The method is a kind of ritual that helps to form the proper mindset so that you can be "in sync with" the current of the objective events or free yourself of preconceptions.

There are a number of methods of divination. A most practical one, which we are going to use, is called the "coin method". In this method, all we need is three coins. Ideally, these should be ancient Chinese coins, with a square hole in the centre. To the ancient Chinese, Heaven is round, and the Earth is square in shape. Thus an ancient Chinese coin embodies the concept of Heaven and Earth. But for practical purposes, any three coins of the same size will do.

In the coin method, one throws the three coins for six times. The first fall of the coins represents the first line (from bottom up). The second fall represents the second line, and so on. The first three lines one gets represent the lower or inner trigram. The other three lines represent the upper or outer trigram. The number of heads or tails decides the nature of the line:

three heads	—— x	old *yang*, a changing line; represented by an undivided line with a cross on the right
two tails	— — ∘	old *yin*, a changing line; represented by a divided line with a little circle on the right
two heads, one tail	——	young *yang*, a stable line; represented by an undivided line
two tails, one head	— —	young *yin*, a stable line; represented by a divided line

A changing line is one that is in the process of developing into a line of opposite nature, i.e. from *yang* to *yin*, or from *yin* to *yang*. A stable line remains unchanged. If all the six lines one gets are stable lines, only the hexagram represented by the lines is to be consulted. If, however, one gets a changing line, an additional hexagram is involved.

For example, if one gets the following six lines:

one should consult Hexagram 55 only. However, if lines 2 and 3 are changing lines, the Hexagram has a tendency to change, and becomes a new Hexagram as follows:

In this case, one should consult Hexagram 55 first, paying particular attention to the changing lines. Then consult Hexagram 54. In this case, Hexagram 55 is called the "Basic Hexagram". It indicates the present situation you are in. Hexagram 54 is the "Transformed Hexagram". It indicates the likely development of events.[18]

VI) How to Read the Translation

The main body of this Translation consists of a translation of the "Judgement" and the Texts of the lines, which are listed under "Conditions". Following the translations is the "Interpretation," which is my own understanding of the most evident messages that the oracle indicates. The purpose of the "Interpretation" is to guide the reader in the beginning stage. Yet such a general "Interpretation", mine or that of any other experts, lacks a vital dimension— you, the diviner. To "personalize" the Hexagrams, the reader is encouraged to read the "Judgement" and "Conditions" carefully and find out how the *Book of Changes* speaks to you personally in its own subtle way.

A reader who is not familiar with the style of the *Yijing* will find it hard to comprehend. Generally speaking, the texts of the "Judgement" and the lines are of two major types: the first type can be called the "omen texts" and the second type "divination texts". The "divination texts" are those which indicate whether the line portends of fortune or misfortune, and the meanings are usually clear to the reader. The "omen texts" are often metaphoric. Sometimes a metaphor is sustained throughout a hexagram. The "dragon" in Hexagram 1 is an example. But sometimes we have different metaphors for different lines, and even different metaphors in one single line. Hexagram 44 is a case in point. A reader who is not aware of this fact may find the texts incomprehensible. The rule of thumb is try not to find a "logical link" between the metaphors. Rather, try to think of the kind of associations they give rise in your mind. Associate the metaphors freely with the persons and events in your life. Imagine the picture, not the logic.

This Translation has benefited much from the expertise of modern Chinese authorities, and is therefore more accurate than most translations which rely too heavily on traditional interpretations alone. A case in point is the word *zhen*, which traditional Confucian scholars interpreted as "perseverance". As the Chinese experts have shown, in most cases, this word should mean "to portend" or "the portent". Failure to understand the nature of the "omen texts" also renders some translations too "logical" to be used for "divination," or as a guide to our own "unconscious".

A final word of caution: do not take the gender and numbers of the nouns in the Translation too rigidly. In the Chinese original, these are not indicated. Therefore, the reader may read "he" as "she," "they" or even "it".

Free your mind from preconceptions and "logics", then you will hear the words of *Changes*.

1. See Liao Mingchun et al, *Zhouyi yanjiu shi,* pp. 36-53.

2. See James Legge, *The Texts of Confucianism, Pt. II, The Yi King* [Yijing]. Oxford, 1899. *SBE* No. 16.

3. See Joseph Needham, "The System of the Book of Changes" in Needham, *Science and Civilisation in China* (Cambridge: Cambridge University Press, 1956), pp. 304-345.

4. See Eleanor B. Morris, *Functions and Models of Modern Biochemistry in the I-ching [Yijing]* (Taipei: Zhongzheng Shuju, 1968).

5. See Fritjof Capra, *The Tao of Physics* (Berkeley: Shambhala, 1975).

6. For a brief summary of various studies on modern science and the *Book of Changes,* see Liao Mingchun et al, *Zhouyi yanjiu shi* [A History of Yijing Studies] (Changsha: Hunan Chubanshe, 1991), pp. 436-440.

7. For example, see Everett Klieinjans, *I Ching [Yijing]—Book of Symbolic Communication* (Singapore: The Institute of East Asian Philosophy, 1989).

8. See Needham, *Science and Civilisation in China,* pp. 340-345.

9. See Fung Yu-lan, *A History of Chinese Philosophy.* Tr. by Derk Bodde (Princeton: NJ: Princeton University Press, 1952), p. 380. See also A.C. Graham, *Disputers of the Tao* (La Salle, Illinois: Open Court, 1989), p. 359.

10. See Carl G. Jung, "Foreword" in Richard Wilhelm, *The I Ching, or Book of Changes.* English translation by Cary F. Baynes (Princeton, NJ: Princeton University Press), pp. xxi-xxxix.

11. See A.C. Graham, *Disputers of the Tao,* p. 369.

12. See A. C. Graham, *Disputers of the Tao,* pp. 368-9.

13. See John Blofeld, *I Ching, the Book of Change* (London: George Allen

& Unwin, 1965), p. 26.

14. See the *Lunyu (Analects)*, 7:21.

15. See Liao Mingchun et al, *Zhengyi yanjiu shi*, p. 26.

16. See *Zhouyi Wang-Han zhu* (Changsha: Yuelu Shushe, 1993), p. 247.

17. *Zhouyi Wang-Han zhu*, p. 247.

18. To locate the hexagrams quickly, please refer to the Hexagram Chart in the appendix located on p. 220 of this volume. This is a modification of the chart in Dong Hengyu, *Zhouyi jingshang shouce* (Beijing: Wangguo Xueshu Chubanshe, 1193), p. 314.

Translation
of the
Sixty-four Hexagrams

Hexagram 1 Qian—The Assertive

 乾 Qian

The Symbols
Outer Heaven/The Assertive
Inner Heaven/The Assertive

The Judgement
A sign of great fortune; an auspicious portent.

The Conditions
Line 1 (yang): A dragon in retreat; don't assert yourself yet.
Line 2 (yang): The dragon appears in the fields; a meeting with the powerful will be rewarding.
Line 3 (yang): A superior man strives forward in the day, and reflects on his moves at night; although you may be in a difficult situation, there will be no harm.
Line 4 (yang): The dragon either leaps upward or stays in the lake; there will be no harm.
Line 5 (yang): The dragon soars high in the sky; a meeting with the powerful will be rewarding.
Line 6 (yang): The dragon soars to the extreme ends of the sky; there will be regrets.
All yang: A host of dragons without a leader; auspicious.

The Interpretation
This is a Time for action. The world belongs to men who are strong-willed yet flexible, ambitious yet prudent. Men of ability must leap at the chance, or they will be left behind.

However, whether an individual will succeed depends also to a large extent on the Timing of his action and the Position he

1《象》曰： 天行健，君子以自强不息。

The way of Heaven is strong. In observing the sign, the superior man strives unceasingly to strengthen himself.

finds or puts himself in. He will have regrets if he asserts himself too early, even though Time rewards the assertive, hard-working and ambitious. A strong man in a low Position should always act with prudence, like a dragon staying deep down in the lake, waiting for its chance. Yet as he climbs to the top of the social ladder, he should boldly manifest his forte and power, thus winning the admiration of his superiors. But going to the extreme and acting in defiance of one's superior or the collected will of one's colleagues will result in regrets.

In such a Time when men of resolution are all contending for power, one should avoid posing as *the* leader, even if one is in the leading position.

In handling your business, be firm and assertive but not antagonistic. Embark on an ambitious plan and expand the horizon of your enterprise, but always open your eyes to the ever-changing situations. Change your plans and Positions accordingly.

You have to reckon with a number of strong-willed persons around you. Appreciate their strong points in accordance with their Positions in relation to yours. Let each and all of them have the chance to demonstrate their worth.

As the Hexagram manifests, there is a Heaven beyond the other. New worlds are waiting for the daring ones to explore. Strong men will always have their match.

Hexagram 2 Kun—Inner Strength

 坤 Kun

The Symbols
Outer Earth/Inner Strength
Inner Earth/Inner Strength

The Judgement
A sign of great fortune. This portends profit for he who has the character of a mare. A superior man travels afar. Though he may be lost in the beginning, he will eventually find his master. A sign of profits. If you go to the West or South, you will make a fortune.[1] If you go to the East or North, you will lose a fortune.[2] An auspicious portent for he who wants to settle down.

The Conditions
Line 1 (yin): A mare treads on thin frost; the ice on the ground will grow thick.
Line 2 (yin): The mare wanders in a vast plain. Though it is not familiar with the plain, it will not be unprofitable.
Line 3 (yin): The mare radiates inner strength;[3] the portent accords with your wishes.[4] You may embark on a big project—though it may not be a big success, the result will be satisfactory.
Line 4 (yin): The mare remains as silent as a tied up sack; there will be no harm, nor will you receive praise.
Line 5 (yin): The mare is dressed up in the auspicious, yellow colour; a sign of great fortune.
Line 6 (yin): The mare fights with a dragon in the fields;[5] its blood spills all over.[6]
All yin: If you are seeking advice on a matter of the distant future, this is an auspicious portent.

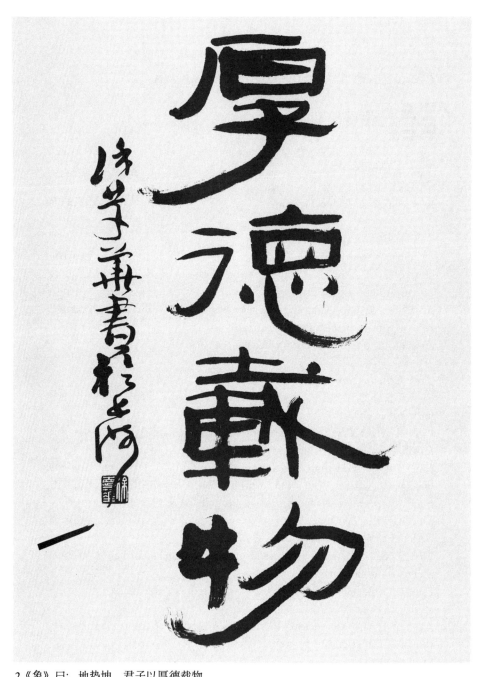

2《象》曰：地势坤，君子以厚德载物。
The way of Earth is receptive. In observing the sign, the superior man cultivates his virtue and carries all.

The Interpretation

The Time has come when one should rely on his stamina and inner strength rather than the exertion of will.

There are difficulties ahead, yet if one moves on carefully and steadily, one will achieve what he wants. If one is familiar with one's turf, one will be able to find his bearings in a vast terrain of divergent landscapes. A Mare will be able to find its home, so a man of inner strength and stamina will eventually find his destination. Yet if he becomes over-confident and forgets that his strength lies in cold determination rather than passionate manifestation of will, he will clash with a strong adversary and meet with disaster.

Make a realistic plan and stick to it. Recognize the strength and weakness of your company. You may expect some long-term profits, but not a windfall. Do not cross the line and enter the turf of a strong competitor.

If you are starting a new career, keep a clear account of your forte and limitations. Choose one that calls for hard-work and perseverance. You may have to endure quite some hardship in the beginning, but your grit will lead you to your destination.

You may now have problems in your personal relationships. Yet with a clear idea of what you want while yielding to the wishes of your partner in minor matters, you will eventually lead your partner out of the icy ground, though the frost will thicken initially. The two of you will settle in your dreamland.

Docility and stamina as symbolized by the Mare are the very qualities you have. Do not lose sight of your forte.

Hexagram 3 Tun—Difficulty

 屯 Tun

The Symbols
Outer Thunder
Inner Rain

The Judgement
A sign of great fortune; an auspicious portent. Do not travel afar. It will be profitable to embark on a big enterprise which you may consider as important as the founding of a kingdom.

The Conditions
Line 1 (yang): A horse trots; this is a good sign for he who wants to settle down; auspicious also for one who wants to embark on a big enterprise.

Line 2 (yin): The horse trots and canters in difficulty. It circles around the same spot. The rider does not come to plunder, but to make a marriage proposal. Yet it is not the time for the girl to get married. She will need to wait for ten more years.[7]

Line 3 (yin): The rider hunts in the hill.[8] Yet without a guide, he will end up wandering in the forest. A superior man, seeing the risk, will rather give up the chase. If he proceeds, he will encounter danger.

Line 4 (yin): The horse trots and canters in difficulty. The rider comes to propose. Move on, this is an auspicious sign; there will be no harm.

Line 5 (yang): The hunter hoards his meats. If you are seeking advice on minor matters, this is an auspicious sign; but if you are seeking advice on important matters, this is an ominous omen.

Line 6 (yin): The horse trots and canters in difficulty; the rider

3 《象》曰：云雷，屯。君子以经纶。

Tun is a sign of rain clouds and thunder. In observing the sign, the superior man embarks on a big enterprise.

weeps; tears of blood drip incessantly.

The Interpretation

This is one of the Hexagrams that is telling of the peculiar philosophy behind the *Book of Changes*. The Hexagram is that of Difficulty, yet the Judgement speaks of great fortune: as every *yang* element has the seed of *yin*, and every *yin* force the potentiality of *yang*, a Difficulty may turn into a chance of success, so long as one acts cautiously and is wary of the Difficulty.

Move on steadily and never lose sight of your objective, then you will eventually accomplish what you want. There are difficulties ahead, and you may have to wait for a long time before you can accomplish your goal. If you are running a small business, grab at every chance of making money as it comes. But if yours is a big enterprise, do not resort to such short-sighted practices as hoarding, or you will suffer loss in the long run.

If you are seeking counsel on marriage/partnership, the advice that the Hexagram gives is apparent. Your prospective bride/partner needs more time, but if you are sincere and have the right person to inform you of her/his background, you will eventually win her/his heart. Do not let any mercenary motive ruin this relationship.

A Time of Thunder and Rain is a Time of Difficulty. Yet plants will have the water to sustain life and start to sprout. With perseverance, one will weather this Thunder and Rain, and grow.

Hexagram 4 Meng—Wild Grass, the Undisciplined

 蒙 Meng

The Symbols
Outer Mountain
Inner Water/Danger

The Judgement
A sign of success. It is not that I seek the unlearned. It is the unlearned who seeks my advice. I will give you my answer at the first oracle. But if you test me again with more oracles, I will consider it a blasphemy. I will not answer the blasphemous. This oracle portends good fortune.

The Conditions
Line 1 (yin): Weed the grass.[9] Punish the undisciplined. If you remove their fetters, you will have regrets.
Line 2 (yang): Bundle up the weeded grass. This is a sign of good fortune. Marry the woman, it will be auspicious. The son will be capable of taking charge of the household.
Line 3 (yin): Do not take the woman by force, or you will meet with armed resistance and may even lose your life. This portends of no long-term profit.
Line 4 (yin): You will be tired out weeding the grass. Misfortune.
Line 5 (yin): Cut the grass. An auspicious sign.
Line 6 (yang): Hack the grass. It will not be advantageous to resort to plundering. Yet it will be advantageous to resist the attack of a plunderer.

4《象》曰：山下出泉，蒙。君子以果行育德。

Meng is a sign of spring water flowing from the foot of a mountain. In observing the sign, the superior man acts with determination in the pursuit of moral cultivation.

The Interpretation

When life begins, there will be an initial stage of Difficulty. One has to weed the Wild Grass to protect the plant. And this has to be done soon, or the job will be too tiresome for one to handle.

Similarly, the wildness in a young child has to be dealt with at an early stage so that the child can grow properly. The reckless child has to be disciplined. However, do not overdo it, for undue harshness will rebound. Be firm and persistent, but not rigidly severe.

If you are launching a new venture, keep an eye on possible trouble makers. Discipline the undisciplined before the situation grows out of control. Once your business is in order and has grown, you may consider merging with another company. Choose someone reliable to take charge of the daily running of your company so that you can concentrate on the merging plan. In this attempt to take over the other company, do not force it, or the symbolic woman will resent your overtures. In this new phase of development in your company, do not lose sight of possible troubles that may sprout, or you will be worn out by internal problems.

For a teacher or a parent, this Hexagram has some good advice. Discipline your child before he grows wild. However, resist the temptation to force your own standard upon the child. Accept and appreciate the worth-commending traits of the child, then he will accept your discipline. Weed the wild grass, but not the flower, in your child.

Water below Mountain symbolizes Danger. Starting a business or embarking on a new phase of development always involves danger. Bringing up a child can also be a "dangerous" job; too little or too much discipline will ruin the child.

Hexagram 5 Xu—Waiting

 Xu

The Symbols
Outer Water/Cloud
Inner Heaven

The Judgement
If you are sincere and steadfast, you will have great success. This is an auspicious portent. It will be profitable to cross the Great Stream.

The Conditions
Line 1 (yang): Waiting in the border. Be patient, and there will be no harm.
Line 2 (yang): Waiting on the sand. There will be some gossips, but in the end everything will be fine.
Line 3 (yang): Waiting in the marsh. The position you take will invite attacks by your enemy.
Line 4 (yin): Waiting in the trench.[10] You will get out of the pit.
Line 5 (yang): Waiting at meat and drink. An auspicious portent.
Line 6 (yin): You have fallen in the pit. Three unexpected guests will appear. Honour them, and there will be good fortune in the end.

The Interpretation
There are Times when one has to Wait, for the desired result, or the beloved person. Meanwhile, there will be gossips or criticism, not because one has done something, but because of the Position one is in. In this Time of Waiting, Patience and Reverence are the unfailing words to observe.

The situation is severe. You are trying to cross the symbolic

饮食宴乐甲戌夏华书

5 《象》曰： 云上于天，需。君子以饮食宴乐。
Xu is a sign of clouds floating in the sky. In observing the sign, the superior man eats and drinks and enjoys himself.

Great Stream, attempting to land on a new world. In doing so, you are in a crisis, financially or otherwise. Wilful actions will bring you no good. All you can do is to Wait, and in the meanwhile Respect all people you have to deal with, even your debtors or former adversaries. With Patience and Respectfulness, you will survive the crisis. Help will come from an unexpected source.

Your relations with your friend is strained, because you demand a further development. There will be rumours about your motive. People will attack you for no reason. But if you are Sincere and Patient, your relations will survive and grow. When the Time ripens, you will be hearing the good news from your friend, while you are at Meat and Drink.

Rain Cloud has gathered in the Sky. Wait and be Patient. The cherished Rain will fall.

Hexagram 6 Song—Litigation

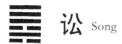 讼 Song

The Symbols
Outer Heaven
Inner Water

The Judgement
Though one may be in the right, he has to remain alert and be cautious. Stop halfway, and there will be good fortune. Pressing it through will bring misfortune. It will be advantageous to meet the man in power, but crossing the Great Stream is not.

The Conditions
Line 1 (yin): Do not pursue the case to the end. There will be some gossips, but there will be good fortune in the end.
Line 2 (yang): You will lose the case. Retreat and hide in a small town of three hundred households. It will not be disastrous.
Line 3 (yin): You will have to live on your inheritance. An ominous portent. But good fortune will come in the end. You may be given the chance to join the King's services; do not claim the merit of any achievement.
Line 4 (yang): You will lose the case. Withdraw and accept the judgement. This oracle portends safety and good fortune.
Line 5 (yang): Go ahead with the case. There will be great fortune.
Line 6 (yang): A leather belt for high-ranking officials will be bestowed on you, yet it will be snatched thrice in a matter of days.

The Interpretation
Every now and then, one may be in conflict with other people and may have to take the case to the court of public opinion

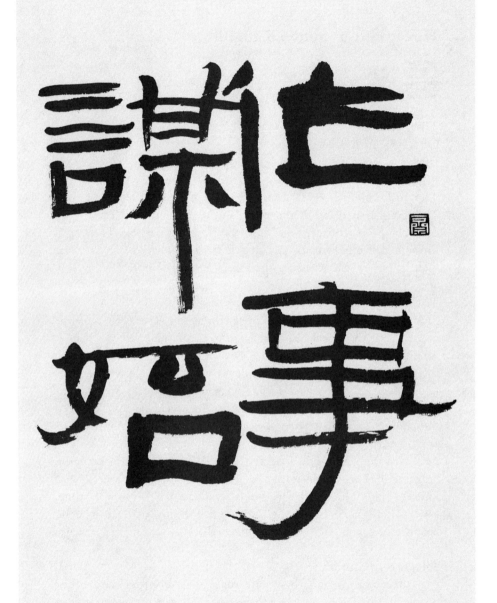

6《象》曰：天与水违行，讼。君子以作事谋始。
Song is a sign of Heaven and Water going their opposite ways. In observing the sign, the superior man tries to avoid litigation, planning carefully right from the very beginning all that he does.

or the court of justice. Though one may win, it is unadvisable to corner one's adversary. Always remember this golden rule of the *Book of Changes*: extreme *yang* will lead to *yin* and extreme *yin* to *yang*. Stop before things develop to the undesirable end.

Someone may have infringed on your interest or violated your rights. Warn him first. If the warning serves its purpose, let the matter settle there. Do not listen to those who urge you to take the case to court. Sue him only if the warning goes unheeded. If he then wants to compromise and compensate your loss, meet with him halfway. Try to settle the case out of court, because you will suffer loss. The initial verdict will be against you, and you will suffer. Though the oracle indicates that you may win the case eventually, it also predicts a loss of fame and honour.

You may have problems with your friend. Settle your differences between yourself. It is foolish trying to get other people to your side. Involving others will be damaging to both of you, whether they are on your side or not.

Do not think of crossing the Great Stream. It will lead you to nowhere.

Hexagram 7 Shi—The Army

 师 Shi

The Symbols
Outer Earth/The Masses
Inner Water/Danger

The Judgement
If you are a revered military leader,[11] this portends good fortune.
There will be no harm.

The Conditions
Line 1 (yin): The army must enforce discipline, otherwise there
will be misfortune. A bad portent.
Line 2 (yang): The leader is in the army. He will be fine. No harm
will come to him. The King will thrice bestow gifts on him.
Line 3 (yin): The army launches an attack. Corpses will be carried
back in the wagon. An ominous omen.
Line 4 (yin): The army retreats.[12] No harm.
Line 5 (yin): The game is in the field. It will be a good move to
capture the intruders;[13] there will be no harm. Give the elder son
the sole command. If his authority is divided with the youngster,
corpses will be carried back in the wagon—an ominous omen.
Line 6 (yin): The Great Lord grants the permission: found a state
and establish your own house. Do not employ men of inferior
morality or ability.

The Interpretation
Conflicts unchecked will escalate into open confrontation
and even war. A highly disciplined army and an experienced,
respected commander are the prerequisites for success in the

容民畜眾 歲在甲戌夏日 海上一齋書

地中有水師 法之章

7《象》曰：地中有水，師。君子以容民畜眾。

Shi is a sign of Water under Earth. In observing the sign, the superior man should be generous to the people and embrace the masses.

battlefield. In delegating his power, the chief must give his chosen one the sole command. Authority divided always leads to disaster.

A military confrontation or a war between your organization and its competitors has broken out. You are chosen to take charge of the counterattack. The first thing you must do is to win the respect of your officers. The support of the Masses is required. Discipline must be strictly enforced. You may suffer an initial setback. Withdraw and wait. When the chance comes, act decisively. Entrust the chosen officer with sole command, or you will suffer great loss.

In the end, you will win and be bounteously awarded. You will be promoted, with a department under your control. In recruiting your staff, put ability and conduct above family ties, or your own career will be ruined. With the support of the Masses, you have won the war and thus the promotion. You will continue to need the support of the Masses to consolidate your own power. In favouritism lies Danger.

This Hexagram has some good advice for coaches of a sports team, for sports competition is, in a sense, a kind of war.

Be alerted, for Danger is imminent. Establish a good relation with the Masses. Then yours will be a victorious Army.

Hexagram 8 Bi—Alliance

 比 Bi

The Symbols
Outer Water/Danger
Inner Earth/The Masses

The Judgement
Auspicious. If you have reverence,[14] this portends great fortune.
People who are in trouble will come to seek your alliance. Those
who come late will have misfortune.

The Conditions
Line 1 (yin): They are sincere; ally with them and there will be no
harm. They are sincere; welcome them with a full bowl of wine.
Eventually something unexpected will happen, but everything will
be fine.
Line 2 (yin): Ally with them who are from among your own circle.
This portends good fortune.
Line 3 (yin): An alliance with the wrong people.
Line 4 (yin): Seek outside alliance; this portends good fortune.
Line 5 (yang): Manifest your willingness to ally with people. When
a King hunts, he will pursue his game from three directions only
and let those in the front escape. Therefore, hunters in the area
will have no reason to complain. Good fortune.
Line 6 (yin): An alliance without a leader. Misfortune.

The Interpretation
Danger comes from outside. Defence lies in a strong Alliance
with people at home or abroad.
This is a Time of general crisis. If you are a political leader,

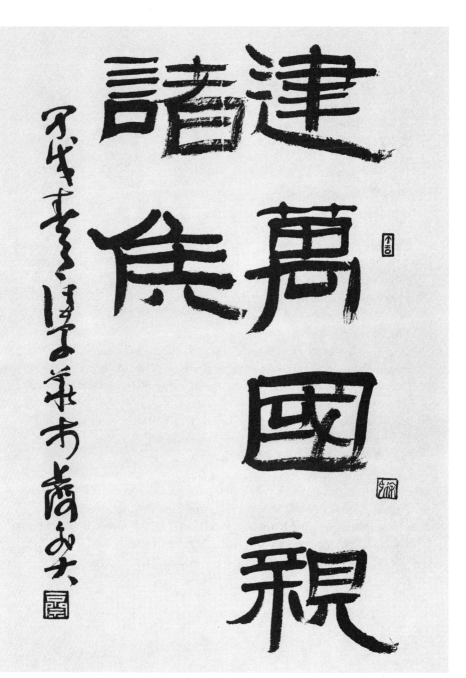

8《象》曰：地上有水，比。君子以建万国，亲诸侯。

Bi is a sign of Water flowing on Earth. In observing the sign, the superior man should bestow the myriad states as feoffs, and ally with the feudal lords.

step out before the situation gets out of hand. People in trouble will come to you for assistance. Lend them your hand, be they from outside or from your own circle, and you will have theirs. You may have the chance to exploit the situation and benefit yourself or your own country. However, do not reap all the benefits. Always leave a share for others in the field. With a sense of commitment, you will lead the country and even the region out of trouble. But if you shrink away, there will be disaster.

This is also a Time of economic recession. Your company is financially strong, though most of the other businesses are weak. Companies in financial crisis will ask for your support. Give them the help, for you will need their help in return in an unexpected crisis. However, be selective in choosing your allies. An alliance with the wrong companies will ruin your own business. Again, you may harvest huge profits, but remember to leave some chances for others.

For a man looking for a prospective bride, this is a highly auspicious oracle. Women will throng you.

The society calls for strong leadership, and the leader needs the support of the Masses.

Hexagram 9 Xiao Xu—Building up Influence

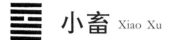 小畜 Xiao Xu

The Symbols
Outer Wind
Inner Sky/Cloud

The Judgement
You will have success. Dense clouds are accumulating at the western border, though there is no rain.

The Conditions
Line 1 (yang): You are returning to your own path. How can there be harm? Auspicious.
Line 2 (yang): Hand in hand with your allies, you come home. Auspicious.
Line 3 (yang): A wheel with its spokes burst out. A quarrel between man and wife.
Line 4 (yin): With sincerity, bloodshed will be averted and fear will disappear. No harm.
Line 5 (yang): With sincerity, you join hands with your neighbours, sharing with them wealth and prosperity.
Line 6 (yang): The rain falls and stops. You will still have a big harvest. This portends danger for women. There will also be misfortune for the superior man who travels abroad on the fourteenth of the lunar month.

The Interpretation
The field is dry. Dense Rain Clouds have accumulated, yet there is no Wind. This is a Time when one has done all he can, having amassed all the resources and support from his camp. Yet

9《象》曰：风行天上，小畜。君子以懿文德。

Xiao Xu is a sign of Wind blowing in the Sky. In observing the sign, the superior man should extol virtue and refinement.

there is one essential factor out of his control.

You have lost your job. Your financial resources have been drained. You have been looking for a job of a different nature. But your applications have been turned down. You sit down and analyse your own strengths and weaknesses. And you decide to land a job in your former field. You have amassed all the information about the companies you want to join, and your networking is well-done. Yet you have not heard from the companies. Your family will be in a difficult time. In such a stressful time, you may quarrel with your spouse. Yet with sincere concern for each other, you will survive. The good news will soon come.

This portends danger for women. If your spouse is looking for a job, what he needs is your care, support and understanding. If you keep on nagging him, your marriage will be in crisis. He has amassed all the resources and support. Give him the time. He will land a new job in his former field, and a better one too.

If you are a businessman who has suffered loss in a new venture, consider returning to your own field. Build up your influence and avoid conflicts with your partner.

If you have followed the suggestion of your business partner to embark on a new venture and have thus suffered loss, do not blame him. Assist him in the revamping of the old business, and with mutual trust and support, your business will recover and prosper.

Dense Rain Clouds have accumulated, and the Wind will come.

Hexagram 10 Lü—Following

 履 Lü

The Symbols
Outer Heaven/A Powerful Ruler
Inner Swamp/His Subjects

The Judgement
You have trodden on the tiger's tail, yet it will not bite. Auspicious.

The Conditions
Line 1 (yang): Follow the way of the pure; there will be no harm.
Line 2 (yang): Follow the way of the righteous; an auspicious sign for the secluded.
Line 3 (yin): A one-eyed man can see; a lame man can walk; yet if he treads on the tiger's tail, the tiger will bite; ominous. This is like an ambitious warrior serving a great ruler.
Line 4 (yang): You have trodden on the tiger's tail; but you are in constant alert and fear; things will eventually be auspicious.
Line 5 (yang): A rash move; this portends danger.
Line 6 (yang): Examine your moves carefully time and again. Highly auspicious.

The Interpretation
Working under a powerful man is like Following a Tiger. A wrong step and one may tread on the Tiger's Tail. Yet if one has not deviated from the proper way, the mighty one will not bite.

You are serving a stern, powerful man of action. This can be Dangerous. Yet Chance always lies in Danger, just as *yang* in *yin* and *yin* in *yang*. Behave yourself, act cautiously and strictly according to the rules and norms, and you will suffer no harm

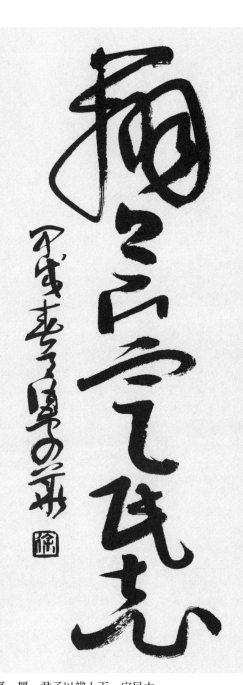

10 《象》曰：上天下泽，履。君子以辨上下，定民志。

Lü is a sign of Heaven above and a Swamp below. In observing the sign, the superior man discriminates the high and the low so as to settle the people's mind.

even if you may have somehow offended your boss. You are competent and confident, and you have your own ambitions. However, do not overestimate your own strength. You do not have the capital to stand on your own feet yet. Though a one-eyed man can see, his vision is still impaired; though a lame man can walk, his movement is still impeded. Any rash move on your part will incur the wrath of your all-powerful boss.

For the modern woman who is married to a man with a strong character and yet wants to have her own career, this Hexagram also offers some good advice. Admittedly, you are intelligent, sharp and have your own ideas. But act prudently, and do not make your husband feel threatened. With tact, you will win his support.

Follow the Tiger. Be on constant alert. The Tiger will not bite without being provoked.

Hexagram 11 Tai—Smooth Interaction

 泰 Tai

The Symbols
Outer Earth/The Subjects
Inner Heaven/The Ruler

The Judgement
The small one will prosper and become great; auspicious and successful.

The Conditions
Line 1 (yang): Pull up the grass, together with weeds of its kind. This portends good fortune and smooth development.[15]
Line 2 (yang): Tolerate the grubbiness and brave the difficulties.[16] Don't forget your distant friends; you may incur a financial loss, but help may come midway.[17]
Line 3 (yang): There is no plain that does not lead to a slope; there is no departing that is not followed by a return. This portends difficulty, though there will be no harm. The traveller will return[18] safely, and will enjoy his food and drink.
Line 4 (yin): A bird soars and flutters—a symbol of a person who does not share his wealth with his neighbours, and one who has not taken any precautions suddenly falls.
Line 5 (yin): The Lord Yi gives his daughter for marriage. Great fortune, highly auspicious.
Line 6 (yin): The wall collapses on the moat. Do not take military action. You will hear orders from town. The portent indicates the coming of troubles.

11《象》曰：天地交，泰．后以财成天地之道，辅相天地之宜，以左右民．

Tai is a sign of the interaction of Heaven and Earth. In observing the sign, the sovereign should observe the ways of Heaven and Earth, complement them with appropriate measures, and in such a way rule the people.

The Interpretation

Everything seems to be upside down: Earth is above Heaven, the yielding, and apparently weak, people have occupied the top Positions while the men of action and strong character are at the bottom. Yet to a man of wisdom, this apparent anomaly is the foundation for further development—the modesty in the leader promotes Interaction.

Outwardly you seem to be weak. However, you have a will of iron inside. You are in a difficult Time. Yet because of your humility, you have maintained good interaction with people below. Therefore, you will be informed of the malpractice among your staff. Act decisively and rectify the situation. As you have maintained a good relationship with all, unexpected help will come from your distant friends, who may even be your former subordinates. The day will come when you are on your feet again.

Always bear in mind that a bird soaring too high will flutter down. Humble yourself, and you will win the heart of your symbolic bride.

Do not be arrogant and militant. Instead, lend your ears to people all around. There will be troubles, and it is only Smooth Interaction with those who are your inferiors that will lead you out of trouble.

The one occupying the Position of Heaven lowers himself to the level of Earth. Then the grass-roots opinion will reach Heaven.

Hexagram 12 Pi—Obstruction

 否 Pi

The Symbols
Outer Heaven/The Ruler
Inner Earth/The Subjects

The Judgement
Obstructed by evil men. This portends misfortune for the superior man. The great one will decline and become small.

The Conditions
Line 1 (yin) Pull up the grass, together with weeds of its kind. This portends good fortune and smooth development.
Line 2 (yin): Tolerate the people who receive orders from above. This portends good fortune for ordinary men, but obstruction for the man in power. Smooth development.
Line 3 (yin): Tolerate the shame.
Line 4 (yang): The order comes; there will be no misfortune. You and your company will have luck.
Line 5 (yang): Be apprehensive of the obstruction, then there will be good fortune for the man in power. Be aware of the impending danger, as if the nation is hanging precariously on a mulberry branch.
Line 6 (yang): Temporary obstruction—there will be obstruction in the beginning but happy endings will come.

The Interpretation
Apparently, this is the way things should be: Heaven at above, Earth down below. The *yang* forces rise and the *yin* forces sink. People occupying the top Positions are strong-minded,

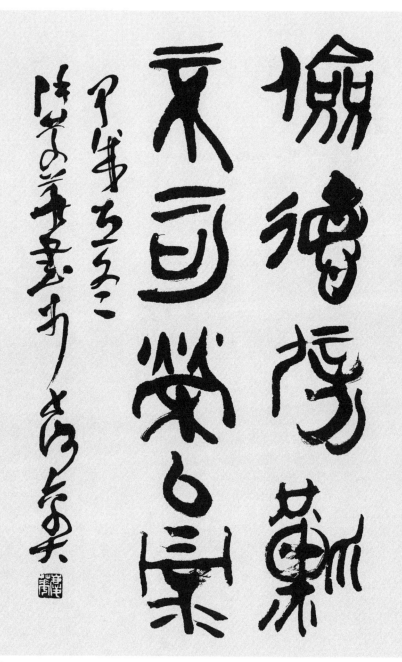

12《象》曰：天地不交，否。君子以俭德辟难，不可荣以禄。

Pi is a sign of non-interaction of Heaven and Earth. In observing the sign, the superior man exercises more prudence to escape danger. He does not take pride in the salary of public office.

maintaining a distance from people below. People down below respectfully accept orders from above.

Yet as the Taoist sage Laozi declares: the tao that can be spoken of is not the Tao. People who maintain a rigid attitude to the "proper order" of things is way off the mark of the Tao of management. Once the Interaction of the *yin* and *yang* forces is Obstructed, the tao will congeal, and it is no longer the Constant and yet Fluid Tao.

You have disciplined the disobedient. You believe that toleration of people below will only be good for an average entrepreneur, not for a top administrator. So far things seem to be running smoothly. Yet your self-imposed distance from the people below has hindered Interaction. The running of the organization will be Obstructed by bad elements at the mid-level. There may come the Time when you have to bear the shame of poor management. With luck, you and your company may survive. Yet if your style of management is not changed, the root of Obstruction will remain. Be apprehensive of the Obstruction. Then you will enjoy long-lasting success.

In your personal relationship, you are isolated without your own awareness. You are gifted, resourceful and determined. You cannot tolerate people who are inferior. Examine your own behaviour, and be more tolerant of others. Remember, an isolated talent will soon find his path to further development Obstructed.

Let the *yang* forces descend and the *yin* forces rise. Interaction is the only prevention against Obstruction.

Hexagram 13 Tong Ren—Joining Forces

 同人 Tong Ren

The Symbols
Outer Heaven/The Ruler
Inner Fire/Brilliance

The Judgement
Join forces at the countryside. The operation will be smooth. It will be advantageous to cross the Great Stream. This portends good fortune for the superior man.

The Conditions
Line 1 (yang): Join forces with your men at the gate. No misfortune.
Line 2 (yin): Join forces with your clan at the ancestral temple, for there will be trouble.
Line 3 (yang): Hide your weapons in the thicket. Climb to the top of the hill. Do not make any move in three years.
Line 4 (yang): Climb up the wall of your enemy. Do not attack yet. Auspicious.
Line 5 (yang): Join forces; your men will first wail and cry out, but will then laugh. All of your companies will meet and combine forces.
Line 6 (yang): Join forces with your men at the suburb. No regrets.

The Interpretation
The Time for a major operation has come. Yet the war will last long and will not be easily won.

This Hexagram is particularly relevant to a military leader whose country is facing imminent attack; and the message is obvious.

13 《象》曰：天与火，同人。君子以类族辨物。

Tong Ren is a sign of Heaven and Fire. In observing the sign, the superior man groups the different clans and makes distinction between things.

However, as with all the Hexagrams of the *Book of Changes*, this one can be taken allegorically. Therefore, the Hexagram speaks to you too.

To a community leader, the Hexagram has this piece of advice: your community is facing a major crisis. Take up the leadership. Organize the community and take the crisis seriously, for even your very heritage is threatened. Yet before you reveal your plan of action, ensure that you have enough resources and support. Collective action is the key to success, and perseverance lays the path to victory. Expect initial setbacks. Your people will suffer hardship. But with concerted effort, you will overcome.

An ordinary citizen who gets this oracle should be alerted to the impending difficulty his family will be in. Gather the family around you. Inculcate in them the importance of the family sticking together in times of hardship.

A Fire has broken out. The community needs a Brilliant Leader to gather the people around to protect the Ancestral Temple.

Hexagram 14 Da You—Great Wealth

 大有 Da You

The Symbols
Outer Fire/Clear Vision
Inner Heaven/Tao of Heaven

The Judgement
Highly successful.

The Conditions
Line 1 (yang): Do not attack each other; then there will be no misfortune, even if you are in difficulty.
Line 2 (yang): A big wagon carrying your gains. There will be opportunities for further development. No misfortune.
Line 3 (yang): The noble one will be invited to the banquet hosted by the Son of Heaven. Those of inferior positions are not.
Line 4 (yang): No boasting of your great wealth;[19] then there will be no misfortune.
Line 5 (yin): Be sincere, accessible, and yet dignified. Auspicious.
Line 6 (yang): Blessings from Heaven; auspicious; no misfortune.

The Interpretation
In this Hexagram, the line occupying the Position of the Sovereign is a *yin* line. All the other lines are of the *yang*. This underlines the importance of humility and receptivity as the qualities in a leader.

As a community leader, you have gathered the community around you to tackle the crisis. In the beginning, the crisis seems to be insurmountable. Stick together, do not blame one another. Then you will win. The community leaders will be lavishly

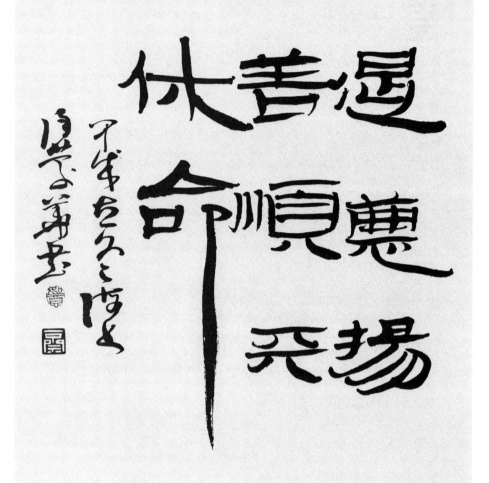

14 《象》曰：火在天上，大有。君子以遏恶扬善，顺天休命。

Da You is a sign of Fire burning in the Sky. In observing the sign, the superior man should suppress the evil and promote the good; thus following the will of Heaven, he should enjoy a good life.

rewarded. But always bear in mind that the war has been won by the whole community, and not you alone. Do not boast of your newly acquired wealth and honour. Remain accessible to your people.

An entrepreneur who gets this oracle has reason to rejoice. Under your leadership, your company has survived a major crisis and has made a huge profit. You will be appreciated by the board of directors and be given a huge bonus. Keep in close contact with your comrades-in-arms. The camaraderie you have is the most important asset to the company.

Keep a Clear Sight of the Tao of Heaven.

Hexagram 15 Qian—Modesty

 谦 Qian

The Symbols
Outer Earth/Depth of Character
Inner Mountain/Outstanding Ability

The Judgement
This indicates success. The superior man will accomplish his task.

The Conditions
Line 1 (yin): The superior man is modest and unassuming. It will be advantageous for him to cross the Great Stream. Auspicious.
Line 2 (yin): Famous[20] and yet modest; an auspicious portent.
Line 3 (yang): Meritorious and yet modest. The superior man will accomplish his task. Auspicious.
Line 4 (yin): There will be no misfortune for he who is courageous[21] and yet modest.
Line 5 (yin): Even the neighbours will suffer loss. It will be advantageous for the superior man to lead the counterattack. No misfortune.
Line 6 (yin): Famous and yet modest; such a person will be successful in his campaigns.

The Interpretation
The country is invaded. This is the Time when it needs a leader who is courageous, accomplished and yet modest. He will lead the nation across the Great Stream.

You are unassuming, famous and accomplished. And above all, you are modest. Your modesty is commendable and have won you the respect of all. However, there are times when one cannot

15 《象》曰：地中有山，谦。君子以捊多益寡，称物平施。

Qian is a sign of a Mountain under Earth. In observing the sign, the superior man takes away from the abundant and adds to those who are poor. He balances things and makes them equal.

afford to be too modest. Your corporation is threatened. Even your business associates will be ruined. Under such an unusual circumstance, you should step out and take the lead. You know clearly what the situation is like. Don't let your usual modesty restrain you from assuming the leadership. You will have the full support of your own staff and that of your associates. You will triumph. Then and only then should you put modesty above other virtues.

On the personal side, you are admired for your humility. And you take pride in it. But at the moment, your adversaries express doubts about your ability. There are gossips about your efficiency. Your colleagues are brought into it too. Do not remain silent. You are the only one who can clear your own reputation and that of your colleagues.

Depth of Character is laudable. But let the Mountain emerge when it is Time.

Hebxagram 16 Yu—The Joyous

 豫 Yu

The Symbols
Outer Thunder/Dynamic Leader
Inner Earth/Obedient Masses

The Judgement
A good sign for the founding of a nation and launching of a campaign.

The Conditions
Line 1 (yin): Famous and joyous; ominous.
Line 2 (yin): He who has a will as firm as a rock would not indulge himself for even one day. An auspicious portent.
Line 3 (yin): He who is sluggish[22] and joyous will have regrets; he who is lazy will also have regrets.
Line 4 (yang): You will have joy in the hunting ground;[23] your quarry will be plentiful. Don't hesitate, for you will surely gain financially as a hair clasp will gather the hair.[24]
Line 5 (yin): This portends illness; yet you will live on for a long time.
Line 6 (yin): The subject of this oracle is deluded by his joy over his success; if he changes, there will be no misfortune.

The Interpretation
A Dynamic Leader with the full support of the Masses will have his plans accomplished. Yet he must guard against smug satisfaction, or he will lead the nation into a long recession.

The people you are working with have long been accustomed to the rules and somehow lack vitality and originality. They will

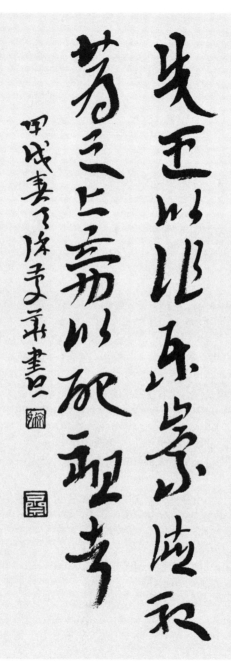

16 《象》曰: 雷出地奋，豫。先王以作乐崇德，殷荐之上帝，以配祖考。

Yu is a sign of Thunder striking and Earth shaking. In observing the sign, the ancient kings made music to eulogize the spirits. Splendid were their offerings to the Lord, and equally grand their sacrifices to their august ancestors.

do whatever you want them to, and never query your decisions. If you yourself are full of ideas and are dynamic, such an obedient following who will not challenge your authority may be good. For you can make up a plan, and rest assured that your orders will be carried through. Nevertheless, there is always another side to the coin.

At the moment, your analysis of the market is correct. Don't hesitate, your company will gain a bounteous profit.

However, the Hexagram also portends danger. Your newly gained success will enhance your status in the company. If you overjoy in your own success, the company will soon suffer, for without your words, your staff will not take any initiative, even if something went wrong. But if you yourself are on constant alert, things will turn out fine.

In the family, you are the one to make all the decisions. Your spouse will submissively agree to whatever you say. Right now, you may gain in the stocks or other kinds of investment. But do not put all your eggs in one basket. Ask for your spouse's opinion. He/she may have some good suggestions, though you will have to make the final decision.

The Thunder roars, the Earth echoes. May the Thunder not strike wrong.

Hexagram 17 Sui—Alignment

 随 Sui

The Symbols
Outer Lake/Happiness
Inner Thunder/Activity

The Judgement
Highly auspicious; a good portent; no misfortune.

The Conditions
Line 1 (yang): The government will issue the permits. A good portent. Travellers will have success.
Line 2 (yin): If you cling to the young guy, you will lose the able man.[25]
Line 3 (yin): If you cling to the able man, you will lose the young guy. If you follow the able man, you will gain what you want. This portends good fortune for one who wants to settle down.
Line 4 (yang): If you align with him just for material gains, then this portends misfortune. Yet if you are sincere, virtuous and know how to behave yourself, there will be no harm.
Line 5 (yang): Sincerity and virtue bring good fortune.
Line 6 (yin): Capture his heart, and strengthen the bonds. Then you can enjoy your success like a king at the western hill.

The Interpretation
There are Times when one has to take the initiative to find one's own Happiness. One has to make sure what he wants before he can make the right decision in the choice of a partner.

For a businessman, this Hexagram portends success in an overseas enterprise. The documents you have been waiting for will

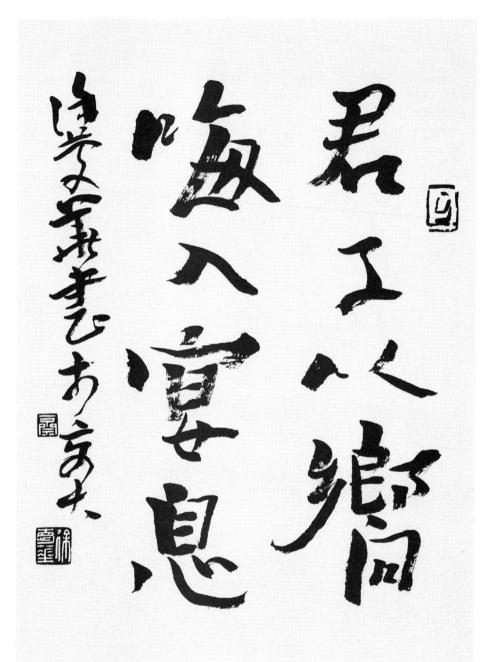

17 《象》曰：泽中有雷，随。君子以向晦入宴息。

Sui is a sign of Thunder roaring over a Swamp. In observing the sign, the superior man will, when the night falls, retire and take a good rest.

be issued. There are two companies you can join in your new venture. You have to choose one of them. Align with the larger and established one. Don't be misguided by short-term profits and ruin your credit in the long run. Let honesty and sincerity be your watchwords in all your dealings with your partners. Once you have won their confidence, you can sit back and reap your profits.

As much as to a businessman, this Hexagram also speaks to someone who is looking for a mate. You have two persons to choose from. One is a young man of your own age. The other is a mature man with a successful career. Let your heart be your guide. Sincerity and virtue brings good fortune. But if your choice is made out of mercenary calculations, you will suffer. Only with your heart can you win his heart. Once you have captured his heart, you will be on cloud nine.

When the Thunder strikes, the Lake stirs.

Hexagram 18 Gu—[The Parents] Enterprise[26]

 蠱 Gu

The Symbols
Outer Mountain
Inner Wind

The Judgement
Highly auspicious. It will be profitable to cross the Great Stream, though you must do so within seven days starting from the eighth day of this ten-day week to the fourth day of the next ten-day week.[27]

The Conditions
Line 1 (yin): Carry on the work of your father. As this is done out of filial piety, there will no misfortune. Though it is dangerous, everything will be fine in the end.
Line 2 (yang): Carry on the work of your mother. You should not try to seek to know whether this portends fortune or misfortune.
Line 3 (yang): Carry on the work of your father. There will be some regrets, though nothing serious will occur.
Line 4 (yin): You act too slowly to carry on the work of your father. If you progress in this manner, you will have troubles.
Line 5 (yin): Carry on the work of your father, and you will acquire a good reputation.
Line 6 (yang): Do not join the services of the king. Set yourself a higher goal.

The Interpretation
One has his own career. Suddenly, one's parent retires or passes away, and one is to carry on the family enterprise, or it will

18 《象》曰：山下有风，蛊。君子以振民育德.

Gu is a sign of Wind blowing below a Mountain. In observing the sign, the superior man provides reliefs to the people, and cultivates his virtue.

close down. Very often, one wonders whether he should give up his own job.

Boldly shoulder the responsibility of carrying on the family enterprise. In your society, your filial piety will win you a good name. There may be some risks and you may encounter some setbacks. At times, you may even wonder whether you should have given up your own career and interest. In the end, you will find satisfaction in your new accomplishment. Don't hesitate, take up the work now. Procrastination will only make your work more difficult. You will be so successful as an entrepreneur that someone may even urge you to try your hand at politics. Resist the temptation, for you will fare much better in the business world. Once you reach the top, you will enjoy the scene.

The responsibility is as colossal as a Mountain. The moral obligation is equally heavy. Like a Wind blowing in diverse directions, one wavers. Yet the Wind blowing up the hill will eventually reach the top.

Hexagram 19 Lin—Approaches to Ruling

 Lin

The Symbols
Outer Earth/Soil/The Country
Inner Lake/Water/The People

The Judgement
Highly auspicious. This portends good fortune. But when the eighth month comes, there will be danger.

The Conditions
Line 1 (yang): Rule by education and persuasion.[28] This portends good fortune.

Line 2 (yang): Rule with leniency.[29] Auspicious; no misfortune.

Line 3 (yin): Ruling with a heavy hand[30] will not bring long-term profits. Be wary of this, then there will be no misfortune.

Line 4 (yin): Take charge personally; no misfortune.

Line 5 (yin): Rule with wisdom, as is appropriate for a great lord. Auspicious.

Line 6 (yin): Rule with sincerity and forbearance; auspicious; no misfortune.

The Interpretation
Though one speaks of different Approaches to Ruling, heavy-handed practices should be avoided. If the situation demands the use of force and suppression, one should always keep in mind the danger of such practices. When things return to normal, leniency and forbearance should reign. For as the Taoist master Laozi teaches, the Supple and Soft is superior to the Strong and Stiff.

If you are a minister or an administrator, the message of this

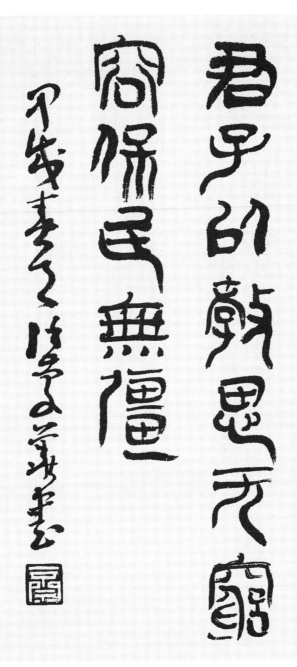

19《象》曰：泽上有地，临。君子以教思无穷，容保民无疆。

Lin is a sign of Earth on a Lake. In observing the sign, the superior man spares no efforts in the education of his people. Embracing and protecting them, he will achieve boundless merits.

Hexagram is obvious. In Times of peace and order, if the public fails to understand your policy, educate them and persuade them. Coercion will only result in resentment. When the majority is law-abiding, leniency shown to the unruly few will win you the hearts of the multitude so that when you may have to resort to heavy-handed measures at Times of national crisis, they will understand. At such a time, you have to take personal charge. And always be wary of the possibility you may have used up this reservoir of support. When the crisis is over, let forbearance rule the day.

The Hexagram also speaks aloud to teachers and parents. An unruly child may need to be severely dealt with. But what the child needs is your care and concern. He will feel it if you express your love in an appropriate way.

The Soil needs to be moistened before plants can grow. And be sure to store up enough Water, for when Summer comes, there will be a drought.

Hexagram 20 Guan—Observation

 观 Guan

The Judgement
The worshipper has washed his hands, and is yet to make the offering. He holds up his head, with sincerity and reverence.

The Symbols
Outer Wind
Inner Earth

The Conditions
Line 1 (yin): A childish view; there will be no misfortune for the ordinary man; but for a superior man, this portends trouble.
Line 2 (yin): A view through the crack of the door; this is a good portent for women.
Line 3 (yin): Observe the life of your own people and decide on what measures to take.
Line 4 (yin): Observe the glorious achievements of the nation. You will have good fortune serving the king.
Line 5 (yang): Observe the life of your own people. There will be no misfortune for the superior man.
Line 6 (yang): Observe the life of their people. There will be no misfortune for the superior man.

The Interpretation
There is a Time for everything. A Time to act, and a Time to halt. This is a Time when one should stop, and Observe carefully before making further moves.

At this juncture of your life, you have an important decision to make. You are pondering over what you should do. You look

20 《象》曰：风行地上，观。先王以省方，观民，设教.

Guan is a sign of Wind blowing over Earth. In observing the sign, the superior man visits his states, observes the people, and then gives them his instructions.

up the *Book of Changes* for advice. But the Hexagram gives you this counsel: with the deep reverence you have as you are making offerings to the gods, observe the life of your own people and the life of other people, then you will find your own answer. In making your observation, always bear in mind your Position and your Identity. An ordinary man can afford to have a simplistic view and act accordingly. A person who has only his own family to take care of can afford to look at just a tiny corner of the society. But for a man of your position, you must have a much broader perspective.

Observe in particular the achievements of the country. Then you will find confidence in your career in the civil services. Compare the life of your own people with the life of the country in your mind, then you will be able to make the correct decision.

The Wind blows over every corner of the Earth. Which corner does the Wind blow most softly?

Hexagram 21 Shi Ke—Biting/ Law Enforcement

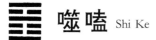 噬嗑 Shi Ke

The Symbols
Outer Fire/Lightning
Inner Thunder

The Judgement
Success; this portends good results in the enforcement of the Law.

The Conditions
Line 1 (yang): The fetters will only cover[31] one's toes. No danger.
Line 2 (yin): Taking a bite off soft meat, one's nose is covered. No danger.
Line 3 (yin): Taking a bite off cured meat, one is poisoned. There will be some troubles, though no danger.
Line 4 (yang): Taking a bite off the flesh dried on the bone, one finds a bronze arrow head. This portends fortune in a difficult situation. Auspicious.
Line 5 (yin): Taking a bite off dried meat, one finds a gold arrow head. This portends hardship, though there will be no misfortune.
Line 6 (yang): The cangue covers one's ears; ill fortune.

The Interpretation
With three *yin* lines sandwiched between two *yang* lines, this Hexagram looks like a Mouth, and thus signifies Biting, which in turn symbolizes Law Enforcement. Law Enforcement always involves two sides: those who break the Law and those who enforce the Law.

When one does not have a job, one may be tempted to win his bread by illegal means. For minor offences, one may only receive

21《象》曰：电雷，噬嗑。先王以明罚敕法。

Shi Ke is a sign of Lightning and Thunder. In observing the sign, the ancient kings defined clearly their penalties so as to establish law and order.

light punishment. Sometimes, one may even escape justice and find a fortune in illegal activities. Yet before long, one may end up in jail. Therefore, one has to think twice before doing anything foolish for the Law will prevail.

Those enforcing the Law must also take heed of what the Law bites. If people living below the subsistence level have to resort to illegal means for food, the law enforcers should restrain from biting too hard. Otherwise, they will end up biting bones, or even metals. When a large number of people have cangues covering their ears, it portends ill fortune, not only for the offenders, but also the nation.

Look before you Bite.

Hexagram 22 Bi—Adornment[32]

 贲 Bi

The Symbols
Outer Mountain
Inner Fire/Blooming Flowers

The Judgement
Success; go ahead, and you will have luck.

The Conditions
Line 1 (yang): Their toes adorned, they would rather go on foot than on carriage.
Line 2 (yin): They trim their beard.
Line 3 (yang): They adorn themselves, and behave themselves; this portends good fortune in the long run.
Line 4 (yin): Adorned in white; speeding ahead on white horses, they do not come to plunder. They come to receive the bride.
Line 5 (yin): They adorn her garden. They do not have enough silk ribbon. There will be trouble, though everything will be fine in the end.
Line 6 (yang): They adorn in white; no misfortune.

The Interpretation
This is a Time of joy and celebration. One's effort is crowned with success.

This Hexagram refers particularly to marriage. Your passion and tenderness will win you the heart of your bride. Your friends and relatives, all dressed up, will come to join you in the wedding ceremony. The bride is waiting. She will show you her most beautiful look when you come. Go ahead, and you will succeed.

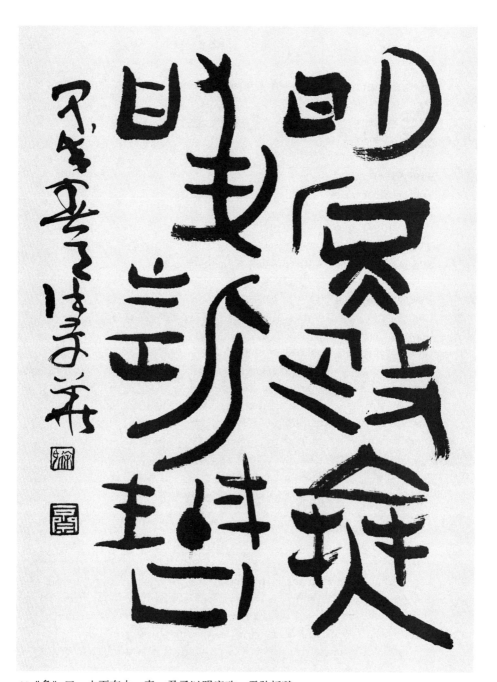

22 《象》曰：山下有火，贲。君子以明庶政，无敢折狱。

Bi is a sign of Fire under a Mountain. In observing the sign, the superior man will make every effort to understand all kinds of issues, and in judging he does not abuse his authority.

White is the colour of purity. You are pure in heart, and so will be your bride.

As for your career, you will find pleasure in your job. Conduct yourself in a noble manner. Pay attention to your look. Always dress properly. Work efficiently, and yet with grace. Make your office a joyful place to work, and adorn the relationship with your colleagues with the flower of sincerity. Claim only the merits that are rightfully yours and don't steal others' credits. Adorn your outstanding performance with the flower of honesty. With an unblemished record and the emotional support of your co-workers, you will take home the symbolic bride.

Flowers are blossoming all over at the foot of the Mountain. Let there be laughter and joy.

Hegagram 23 Bo—Falling Apart

 剥 Bo

The Symbols
Outer Mountain
Inner Earth

The Judgement
Not a good portent for travelling afar.

The Conditions
Line 1 (yin): In the dream,[33] the feet of the bed fall apart. This portends ill fortune.
Line 2 (yin): In the dream, the board of the bed falls apart. This portends ill fortune.
Line 3 (yin): Let it fall apart; no trouble.
Line 4 (yin): The cover of the bed falls apart. Misfortune.
Line 5 (yin): One by one, the court ladies come to seek favour. No misfortune.
Line 6 (yang): A single large fruit remains uneaten. The superior man will gain a carriage; the ordinary men's huts will fall apart.

The Interpretation
This is a Hexagram about a dream. Dreams are often portentous. They reveal to the dreamer the hidden meaning behind all the complexities of the reality that his Unconscious has figured out for him. They also reveal to the dreamer his future prospects. Like oracles, Dreams are often metaphoric. And in this case, the dream becomes an oracle.

You will be facing a very difficult Time. Things will deteriorate and get worse. Do not start any new ventures, for you

23 《象》曰：山附于地，剥。上以厚下安宅。

Bo is a sign of a Mountain sliding down the Earth. In observing the sign, the sovereign should bestow favour on the people, and let them live a peaceful life.

will need all the resources you have to deal with the impending crisis. Various sectors of your business will be affected. You have to weigh the importance of the various sectors and give up the less important ones. Concentrate on rescuing your single important business. In such a time, your employees and business associates will also be affected. Do not forsake them. Give them what they deserve. In the end, they will be the ground on which you will reestablish your enterprise, and it will be a more solid one too.

This is also a difficult Time for your personal relationship. You and your loved one quarrel over all kinds of things. Both of you feel miserable. Yield to him/her as far as you can. Let him/her know the single most important thing—your love remains unchanged. And when the Time comes, the one factor which hinders a reconciliation will be gone. And your relationship will fall, on safe ground.

The Mountain is eroding. Yet the soil will accumulate on the ground.

Hexagram 24 Fu—Returning

 复 Fu

The Symbols
Outer Earth
Inner Thunder/The Dynamic

The Judgement
Success. Whether you stay home or go on a trip, there will be no misfortune. You will gain financially without encountering any trouble. If you go on a trip, you must return in seven days. It is profitable to travel long distance.

The Conditions
Line 1 (yang): Returning without going too far; nothing to regret. Highly auspicious.
Line 2 (yin): The admirable one returns; auspicious.
Line 3 (yin): Going and returning repeatedly; though you will encounter difficulties, there will be no misfortune.
Line 4 (yin): You return alone in the middle of the journey.
Line 5 (yin): You return after much introspection;[34] nothing to regret.
Line 6 (yin): If you go astray and fail to return, there will be misfortune. It will be disastrous. If you launch an expedition, you will suffer a great defeat in the end; even the king will be in trouble. You will not be able to rise again in the next ten years.

The Interpretation
One has experienced something new. But the Time has come when he should stop and resume his former self, or he will suffer great loss.

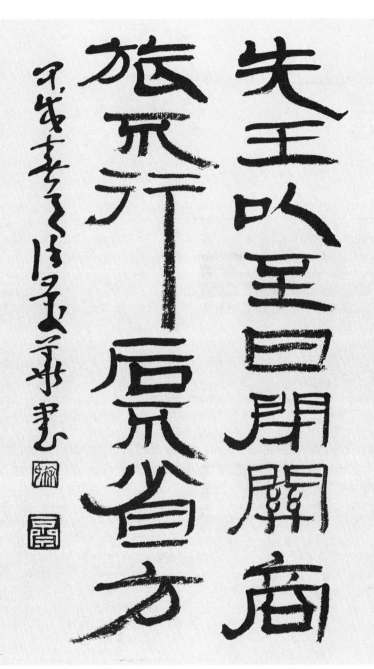

24《象》曰：雷在地中，复。先王以至日闭关，商旅不行，后不省方。

Fu is a sign of Thunder roaring underneath Earth. In observing the sign, the ancient kings, at the time of winter solstice, closed the passes, and would not admit travelling merchants. Neither would they themselves travel through the feudal states.

You are young, smart and dynamic. So you do not want to take the ordinary path. You want to do something people won't usually do. It will be a rewarding experience. But you must not go too far. Resume normal life before it is too late. Or you will go astray. Even your parents will suffer. Ten whole years will be wasted. And ten years is too much time for a young man to waste.

For a businessman in difficulty, the Hexagram has this to say about your recovery: you have embarked on a new venture but cannot find a partner. Do some rethinking. Abandon the project and make a new plan. As long as your credit remains unimpaired, it will help to push your business to a new height. But if you insist on going ahead with this venture alone, your enterprise will be ruined. And you will not be able to recover in the next ten years.

This Hexagram portends good news for one whose relationship has broken. Your loved one will return to you. He/she has suffered much and decides to come back to you. Restrain from blaming him/her, or the relationship will be ruined again.

Let the Thunder in you touch the ground.

Hexagram 25 Wu Wang—The Unexpected

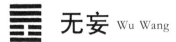 无妄 Wu Wang

The Symbols
Outer Heaven
Inner Thunder

The Judgement
Highly successful. A good portent. Yet if you have evil intentions, there will be disaster. Going too far will result in misfortune.

The Conditions
Line 1 (yang): Proceed without unrealistic expectations; auspicious.
Line 2 (yin): If one could reap without ploughing, harvest without cultivating, then you may go ahead and make profits.
Line 3 (yin): An unexpected trouble. The tethered cow is carried off by a passerby, and the villager suffers.
Line 4 (yang): A good portent; no misfortune.
Line 5 (yang): You have fallen ill unexpectedly; but you will recover without taking medicine.
Line 6 (yang): Something unexpected will happen; there will be disaster if you go, and you will make no profit in the long run.

The Interpretation
Life is full of surprises. From time to time, one tends to believe in Luck. Lucky he may sometimes be, but if he left everything to Luck, he would have trouble.

You have come up with a splendid idea and want to start a new project. Go ahead if you are prepared to work hard for it. But you must not leave things to others, expecting them to fulfil the task for you. Be prepared for the unexpected. You may be

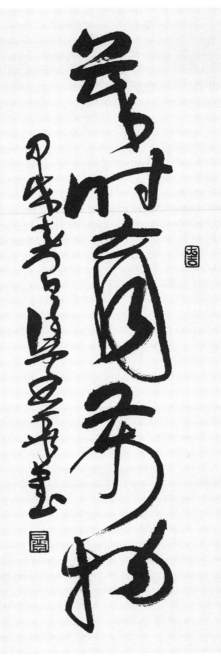

25 《象》曰：天下雷行，物与，无妄。先王以茂对时育万物。

Wu Wang is a sign of Thunder roaring under the Sky, and of the myriad things springing to life. In observing the sign, the ancient kings strived to keep in harmony with the Time. They fostered and nourished all beings.

implicated in someone else's wrongdoing. Conduct yourself properly, then there will be no harm. You may fall ill unexpectedly. You will recover, but the job has to be continued while you are recovering. Arrange to have a reliable colleague to cover your duties if this does happen. If you are thus prepared, you will succeed. If you are not, then when something unexpected occur, you will be stricken down.

Something may be stolen from you. You house may be affected in a fire which breaks out because someone else is careless. But if you have insurance, it will not be disastrous.

A student who gets this Hexagram should stop playing smart. Do your homework and study hard if you want to have good results. One has to plough before he can harvest.

The Thunder strikes. No one knows when it will strike.

Hexagram 26 Da Xu—Building Up Great Strength

 大畜 Da Xu

The Symbols
Outer Mountain/Restrain
Inner Heaven/Sun/Power

The Judgement
This portends good fortune. You do not need to eat into your own savings. Auspicious. It is profitable to cross the Great Stream.

The Conditions
Line 1 (yang): There are difficulties; it will be advisable to stop.[35]
Line 2 (yang): The axle of a wheel of the wagon has come off.
Line 3 (yang): A good horse running after the other—this portends good fortune for one who is in difficulty. Practise chariot driving daily. In the long run, it will be profitable to proceed.
Line 4 (yin): A horn guard is tied to a young bull. Highly auspicious.
Line 5 (yin): The wild pig is kept in the sty.[36] Auspicious.
Line 6 (yang): Blessings from Heaven;[37] success.

The Interpretation
The Mountain is blocking the view of the Sun. But Day has come. The Day will become brighter and brighter.

You are moving steadily up. At the moment, your pace is arrested. There is one vital factor that is not favourable to you. Stop and analyse the situation. Devise a new strategy. But do not reveal your ambitious plan before the Time comes. Meanwhile, build up your influence. Recruit to your camp more men of high calibre. Respect your right-hand man, and other competent people

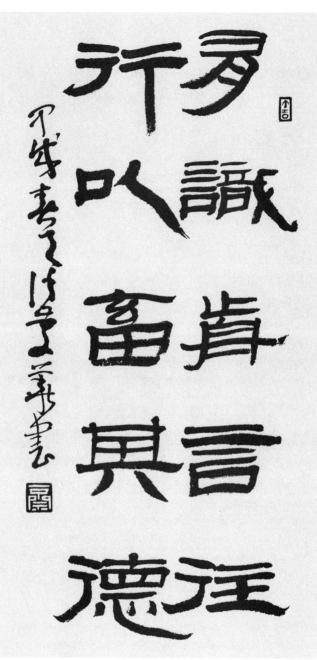

26《象》曰：天在山中，大畜。君子以多识前言往行，以畜其德。

Da Xu is a sign of Heaven in Mountain. In observing the sign, the superior man learns from the words and deeds of ancient sages, and thus nourishes his own virtue.

will be drawn to you, like good horses following a steed. Your power thus built up, the symbolic young bull and wild pig will be yours to capture. You will not only survive the situation but will reach a new height in your career.

For the time being, your relationship with the object of your love does not seem to be making any progress. He/she is not ready to accept your burning passion. Do not reveal your deepest feelings yet. Show him/her your concern and care with tact, and in Time he/she will respond. Love begets love. When the Time is ripe, he/she will crave for the sunshine of your love.

A teacher who gets this Hexagram is having a hard time establishing rapport with the students. Work on one or two of the best students first. In Time the class will follow. Even the trouble makers will appreciate your effort. The "young bull" and "wild pig" will be disciplined.

The Sun will soon rise up in the Sky.

Hexagram 27 Yi—Mouth/Providing Nourishment

 颐 Yi

The Symbols
Outer Mountain
Inner Thunder[38]

The Judgement
An auspicious portent. Observe the proper way to provide nourishment—people have to work for their own provisions.

The Conditions
Line 1 (yang): If you forget your own virtue as symbolized by the Sacred Tortoise and covet the food in other's mouth, there will be misfortune.

Line 2 (yin): You turn to people at the top to feed your mouth. In turning to people up in the summit, you deviate from the proper way.[39] This portends misfortune for advancing.

Line 3 (yin): Deviation from the proper way of providing nourishment portends misfortune. You will not achieve anything for a decade. There will be no profit in the long run.

Line 4 (yin): You turn to those at the top to feed your mouth; auspicious. The Tiger at the top is staring down, but people may still satisfy their craving. No misfortune.

Line 5 (yin): You have deviated from the proper way; stop, then this will portend good fortune. Do not cross the Great Stream.

Line 6 (yang): You follow the proper way of providing nourishment. Despite difficulties, it will be auspicious. Crossing the Great Stream will be profitable.

27《象》曰：山下有雷，颐。君子以慎言语，节饮食。

Yi is a sign of Thunder roaring below a Mountain. In observing the sign, the superior man will be careful with his words, and temperate in eating and drinking.

The Interpretation

One has to work to win his bread. Some people rely on their own ability. Some try to find a easy way out by resorting to flattery or other sorts of underhand dodges . But the Hexagram gives this advice: You have in your world land upon land.[40] Cultivate your own land.

You have been working so hard, but your livelihood has improved little. You are jealous of your colleague who is more successful and want to have his share. The Hexagram, however, warns you of the danger of resorting to underhand dodges. You are intelligent and sharp. Your forecasts of market trends are often correct. So you believe you should replace your more "lucky" colleague and think of bringing him down. In doing so, you will deviate from the proper way. Diverting your attention to the ways of bringing down your colleague will undermine your own gift in market forecasting. In the end, you will be despised by all. But if you concentrate on sharpening your own ability, you will eventually be appreciated by your superior. He will keep a watchful eye on you, but he will give you your proper share.

A young man considering to resort to some "clever" ways to get rich should also take note of this piece of advice:

Do not covet the food in other's mouth.

Take good care of your Sacred Tortoise.

Hexagram 28 Da Guo—Excess

 大过 Da Guo

The Symbols
Outer Swamp
Inner Wind/Wood

The Judgement
The beam of the house sags; it will be advantageous to go ahead with the renovations. Success.

The Conditions
Line 1 (yin): Use white rushes for a mat; no misfortune.
Line 2 (yang): A withered poplar sprouts new leaves; an old man marries a young girl; no misfortune.
Line 3 (yang): The beam sags; danger.
Line 4 (yang): The beam is braced; auspicious. Yet if something else happens, there will be trouble.
Line 5 (yang): A withered poplar blossoms. An old woman takes a young man. No misfortune, nor any praise.
Line 6 (yin): Wading out too deep into the water, which goes over one's head. Danger, yet no misfortune.

The Interpretation
One has to face a lot of pressures in life. Sometimes, the pressure comes from outside. Sometimes one gives oneself too much pressure. One may even invite outside pressure for infringing the norms.

Your company has a long history. Its ways of doing business is already behind Time. Its employees have for too long been accustomed to the rigid rules and practices which have contributed

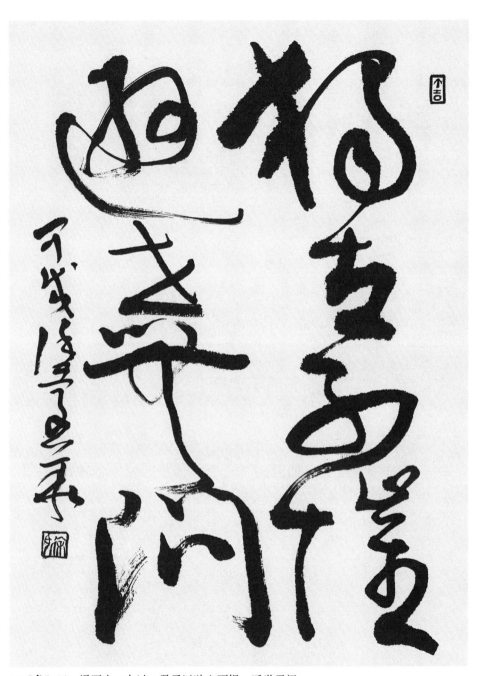

28《象》曰：泽灭木，大过。君子以独立不惧，遁世无闷。

Da Guo is a sign of a Wooden boat capsized in a Lake. In observing the sign, the superior man will stand alone and show no fear. He will live apart from the rest of the world, but he will not be grievous.

to its success. Yet it is the same rules and practices that have begun to sap it of vitality. The Sign has shown that it will be in dire straits, though you do not seem to be aware of it. The board of directors is even talking of taking over a newly established company. If you are not aware of the imminent danger, the day will come when the whole enterprise collapses.

Revamp its organization thoroughly. Brace it with innovative products. Be on constant alert of unexpected dangers. Then the disaster can be averted. The moment you are aware of the Danger, the moment you will be on the way to Safety. Such is the message of the *Book of Changes*.

At the moment, you are facing much pressure from friends and relatives for your relationship with someone much younger. In their opinion, you have gone beyond the norms. Yet for you, this is the belated spring. Though the Hexagram does not advise that you nip this flower of love in the bud, it does urge you to think of the Future, and prepare for it.

The Wooden Boat sails far out in the Lake. Don't overload it, or it will sink.

Hexagram 29 Kan—Abyss

 坎 Kan

The Symbols
Outer Water/Well/Pit
Inner Water/Well/Pit

The Judgement
Sincerity can win people's hearts. You will be successful. Help will come to you.

The Conditions
Line 1 (yin): From a pit to yet another pit, you have fallen into an abyss. Dangerous.

Line 2 (yang): There is danger in the abyss; you can only hope for small gains.

Line 3 (yin): You come to the edge of the pit, which is dangerously deep. You have fallen into the abyss. You will not be able to accomplish anything.

Line 4 (yin): A bottle of wine, a bowl of rice,[41] now contained in an earthen vessel and handed in and out through the window bars of the prison. No misfortune in the end.

Line 5 (yang): The pit is not yet filled, but the mound has been levelled. No misfortune.

Line 6 (yin): Tied up and thrown into the prison for three years without the chance of being released. Dangerous.

The Interpretation
One is aware of a danger, so one tries to avoid it. Yet moving away from one danger he comes to another and falls inadvertently into an abyss. The only rescue comes from outside.

常習

德敦

行事

29《象》曰：水洊至，习坎。君子以常德行，习教事。
Kan is a sign of Water flowing on and on. In observing the sign, the superior man will persist in cultivating virtue, and continue with the good work of educating the people.

So you are in a dire situation. You have just solved one problem, and yet another arises.

Do not panic. Any action taken in hysteria will only get you deeper and deeper into trouble. Analyse the situation and find out what brings about the first problem. Do whatever you can to remedy the situation. But be prepared for the worst. Do not let your pride prevent you from seeking help. If you are sincere, some people will lend you their hand. They will help fill the pit you fall into. You will be out of danger, though minor problems may remain.

For someone who has done something wrong, the Hexagram has this to say: do not try to cover the crime, for in doing so you may make a graver mistake. Seek help from your parents, teachers, friends, or church ministers. If you are truly repentant, they will do their best to, literally or figuratively, "bail you out". But if you continue to solve the problems in your own way, you will end up "behind bars".

There are Pits along the way. Walk with great care.

Hexagram 30 Li—Fire/Fiery Temper

 离 Li

The Symbols
Outer Fire/Fiery Temper
Inner Fire/Fiery Temper

The Judgement
This portends good fortune. It indicates success. Nurture the docility in you, as symbolized by the cow. Auspicious.

The Conditions
Line 1 (yang): Rather than running about in confused steps, deal with it with prudence. No misfortune.

Line 2 (yin): Medium, yellow fire; highly auspicious.

Line 3 (yang): The fire of the setting sun. Unable to receive the approach of old age with equanimity like the ancient sage who beat the pot and sang,[42] an old man bewails. Misfortune.

Line 4 (yang): An outburst, like a huge fire, comes with disasters, like death, like devastation.

Line 5 (yin): After the outburst, one cries a tearful cry, sighs and laments. Auspicious.

Line 6 yang): With his temper thus subdued, the king employs him to launch an expedition. He receives praises for beheading the enemy's chief, sparing those who are not his accomplices. No misfortune.

The Interpretation
One's vigour comes from the Fire of Life. Yet one has to contain the Fire with prudence and docility, or the Fire will become a conflagration that burns all.

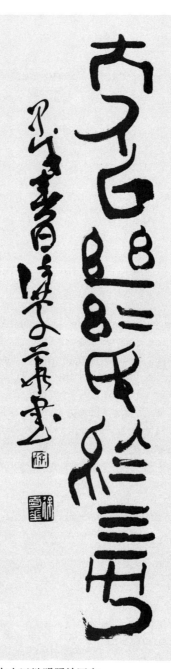

30《象》曰：明两作，离。大人以继明照于四方。

Li is a sign of two Fires. In observing the sign, the great man will continue with his illustrious rule so as to illuminate the four quarters of the world.

You are at the moment very stressful. All things seem to have gone wrong. Your parent, unable to cope with his old age, is always lamenting and adds to your burden. You are about to lose self-control and want to yell it out to everybody. Yet the Hexagram cautions you: nurture the patience and docility in you. Contain your temper. If you make any move in anger, others will react in vehemence. In the end, the Fire will not only burn others—you yourself will be the one who suffers most in the Inferno you yourself created.

Yet do not for this reason put out the Fire, and together with it, the vigour in you. Extreme *yang* is harmful. So is extreme *yin*. Harmonize the Fiery Temper and Docility in you. If you can thus subdue your temper, then you will be appointed to important Positions. Balance between relentlessness to your adversary and leniency to his associates. Then Glory will be yours.

Take note of this: Fire begets Fire.

Hexagram 31 Xian—Move/Influence[43]

 咸 Xian

The Symbols
Outer   Swamp/Young Girl
Inner   Mountain/Young Man

The Judgement
Success. A good portent. Take a girl, it will be auspicious.

The Conditions
Line 1 (yin): She moves[44] her big toes.
Line 2 (yin): She moves her calves; inauspicious. If she settles down, then it will be auspicious.
Line 3 (yang): She moves her thighs and is determined to follow others. If she goes, there will be misfortune.
Line 4 (yang): An auspicious portent. The causes for regret are gone. Coming and going, your friends will follow your plans.
Line 5 (yang): She shrugs; nothing to regret.
Line 6 (yin): She moves her jaws, cheeks and tongue.

The Interpretation
The Time has come when one wants to take a life partner. But before the prospective partner will come, one has to move her/his heart. And she/he will be moved, not immediately, but slowly.

This is primarily a Hexagram about marriage. You have found your Snow White. Yet so far she has not responded to your romantic overtures. And she seems to have someone else in her heart. In the beginning, she is more attracted to the other guy. And if she takes the initiative to approach the man, your dream

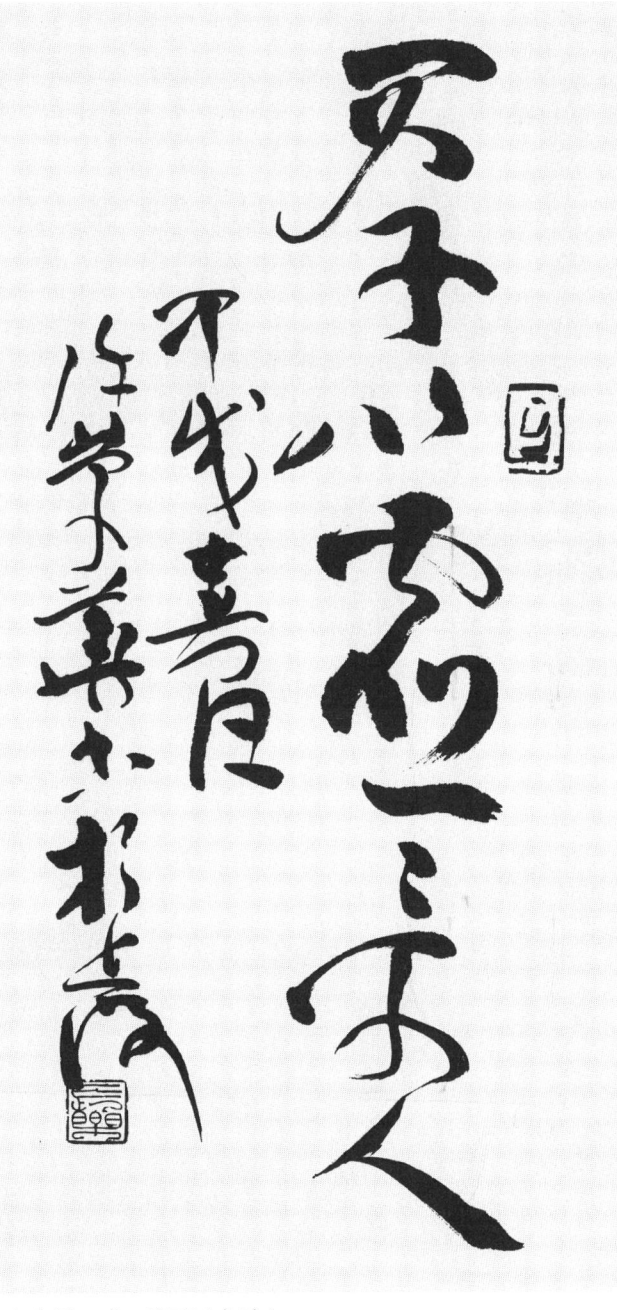

31 《象》曰：山上有泽，咸。君子以虚受人。

Xian is a sign of a Lake on top of a Mountain. In observing the sign, the superior man will humble himself and is receptive to his people's ideas.

will be dashed. Yet as long as she remains undecided, you will have a good chance. If you persist with tact and with the support of your friends, you will see the day when she eventually responds and gives her consent. The thing to remember is this: try to *move*, and not force upon, her. As all the three lines in the inner trigram correspond with all the three lines in the outer trigram, modify your behaviour and mood so as to be in tune with hers. Then Snow White will respond to your kisses.

Those looking for a business partner should also take note of this: a *yang* force repels a *yang* force; so will a *yin* force reject a *yin* force. As *yin* and *yang* complement each other, complement your partner's needs, instead of competing with him in his force. Harmonious and mysterious, such is the Harmony of *Yin* and *Yang*.

Hexagram 32 Heng—Constancy

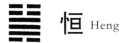 恒 Heng

The Symbols
Outer Thunder
Inner Wind

The Judgement
Success, no misfortune. This portends good fortune. It will be profitable to proceed.

The Conditions
Line 1 (yin): Demanding too much of the partner's constancy. An inauspicious portent. No profits in the long run.
Line 2 (yang): The causes of regret are gone.
Line 3 (yang): Inconstancy will produce shame. This portends misfortune.
Line 4 (yang): There is no game in the field.
Line 5 (yin): Constancy in one's virtue. In a woman, this portends good fortune; but in a man, it portends misfortune.
Line 6 (yin): Shaking the principles of constancy;[45] misfortune.

The Interpretation
The end of one stage always leads to the beginning of a new one. Such is the principle of *Changes*.

If you are seeking advice on your marriage, the message of the Hexagram is clear: you are happily married. Yet your social life has to continue. You still need to interact with other women. Yet your wife seems to lack confidence in you and demands that you spend all of your free time with her. The thought that it may have been better to remain single even crosses your mind. Tolerate

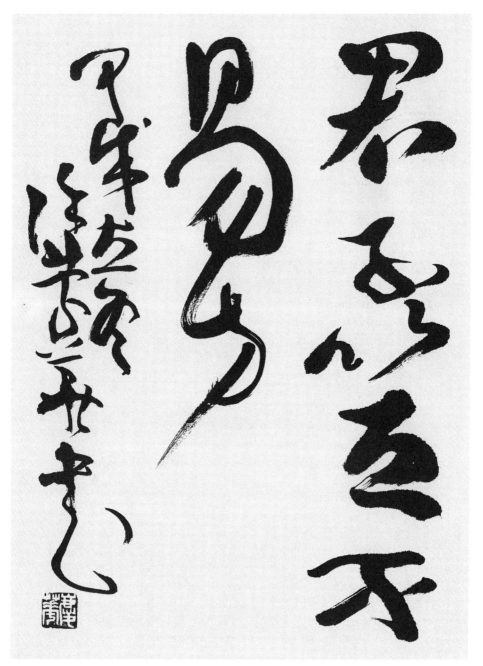

32 《象》曰：雷风，恒。君子以立不易方。

Heng is a sign of Thunder and Wind. In observing the sign, the superior man will stand firm and will not change his principles.

with her. Explain to her why you have to be going out with people. With patience and sincerity, you will make her understand. Yet do not betray her. For inconstancy will lead to disaster in the family. And in the end, you will have no one else, for "there is no game in the field".

A woman who gets this Hexagram should also remember this: demanding too much of your husband's constancy will drive him to inconstancy, for extremity always leads to opposite results. Have faith in him; give him the freedom, and he will constantly be yours.

To one who is seeking advice on his partnership, the Hexagram has this to say: treachery will shake the partnership; and so will be undue demand on loyalty. For a small business, Constancy is a virtue; for a large corporation, *constant* Constancy will hinder progress.

The Thunder strikes, and the Wind follows. In this lies the Constancy of *Changes*.

Hexagram 33 Dun—Retreat

 遁 Dun

The Symbols
Outer Heaven
Inner Mountain

The Judgement
Success; quite an auspicious portent.

The Conditions
Line 1 (yin): This portends danger for the last one to retreat. Do not proceed.

Line 2 (yin): Once one is held fast with yellow oxhide, there will be no way for him to escape.

Line 3 (yang): Tied, one cannot retreat; this is dangerous, like having a grave illness. At such a time, restrain[46] your own men and women, then it will be fine.

Line 4 (yang): An inclination to retreat. Auspicious for the superior man, misfortune for an ordinary man.

Line 5 (yang): A praiseworthy retreat; this portends good fortune.

Line 6 (yang): Retreat and hide far away.[47] No misfortune.

The Interpretation
One ventured out to the world of chances. The Time has come when one has to retreat to the Mountain of his inner self.

Different factions in your department are contending for power. Many will be involved. Refrain from taking part. For no one will benefit from this confusion. Anyone who fails to retreat in Time will have no way out.

Keep a low profile. Keep your opinion to yourself. If the

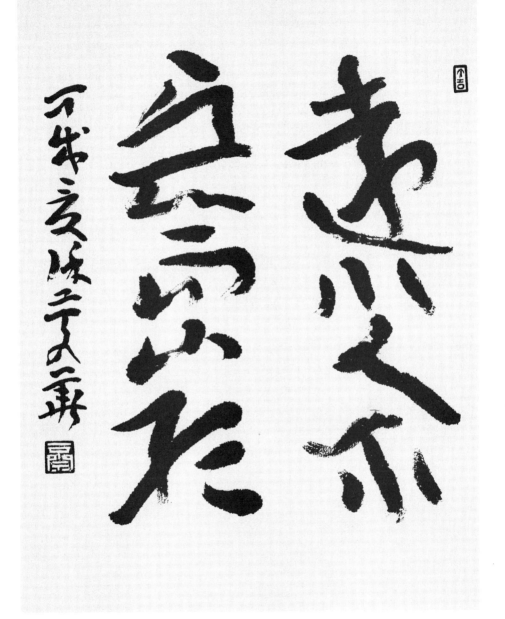

33 《象》曰：天下有山，遯。君子以远小人，不恶而严。
Dun is a sign of a Mountain below the Sky. In observing the sign, the superior man will keep men of low moral standards at a distance. He is firm in this, but he does not act out of spite.

situation is beyond your control and you get entangled without your taking any part, remain calm. Keep a distance from all contending forces. Restrain your own staff from taking part. In Time, your non-involvement will be appreciated by all. Unfortunately, if you are just a low-ranking officer, you will be in a dilemma. Taking part portends no fortune. Yet if you do not take sides, you will be rejected by all. So be prepared for the worst.

This is also a hard Time for businessmen. Competition is becoming increasingly fierce. Consider a strategic retreat. Do not put in more capital.

You may be involved in a complicated relationship. Withdraw before you are tied down.

There is a Time for everything. And now it is the Time to Retreat.

Hexagram 34 Da Zhuang—Great Strength

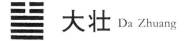 大壮 Da Zhuang

The Symbols
Outer Thunder
Inner Heaven

The Judgement
An auspicious portent.

The Conditions
Line 1 (yang): One begins to acquire strength and feels it in the toes. Yet advancing will bring misfortune, though one may have confidence.
Line 2 (yang): An auspicious portent.
Line 3 (yang): The ordinary man uses physical strength, but the superior man uses a net. This portends danger: a goat butts against a fence and gets its horns entangled.
Line 4 (yang): This portends good fortune. The causes for regret are gone. The fence is broken and the goat's horns disentangled; it is as strong as a large wagon with a strong axle.
Line 5 (yin): The goat disappears in the fields.[48] No misfortune.
Line 6 (yin): The goat butts against a fence, it can neither retreat nor move on. There is no good fortune, but if one realizes the difficulties he is in, everything will eventually be fine.

The Interpretation
Great Strength does not come from physical power. Nor does it lie in a blind exertion of will. A strong man is one who has a clear understanding of the Time and proceed or retreat accordingly.

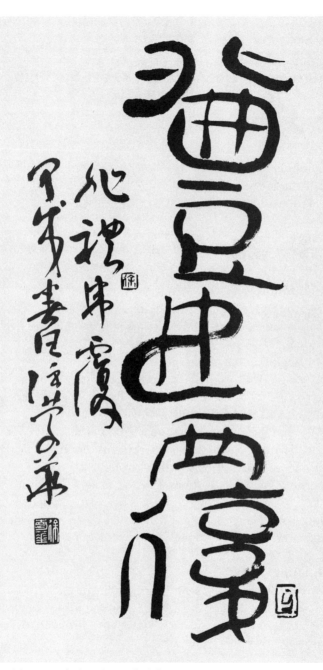

34 《象》曰：雷在天上，大壮。君子以非礼弗履。

Da Zhuang is a sign of Thunder roaring in the Sky. In observing the sign, the superior man will not tread on paths that deviate from the norms.

You have just been promoted to a Position of some power. You like the feeling of it. You want to embark on a bigger project to prove your ability. Think twice before you make any move. Build up your influence before you act. Cast your net of relations wide. Nurture your inner strength before you make a major show of power. Otherwise you may be like the goat whose horns got entangled butting against a fence. Once you have accumulated enough support, you will be able to push down all the obstacles. The important thing is for you to analyse the situation and figure out the possible problems you may encounter, ascertain the nature and complexity of the task in hand, and the kind of resources and support you can get. When the Time comes, strike with full might.

The Thunder is roaring in the Sky. When it strikes, it strikes with Great Power.

Hexagram 35 Jin—Advancement

 晋 Jin

The Symbols
Outer Fire/Sun
Inner Earth

The Judgement
He is a vassal who has contributed to the prosperity and stability of the empire. The king therefore bestows on him thousands of horses and receives him three times in a day.[49]

The Conditions
Line 1 (yin): You will be promoted, and promoted to the top. An auspicious portent. Though you may not have won the confidence of all, there will be no harm.

Line 2 (yin): You will be promoted. Though there will be trouble ahead, this portends good fortune. You will receive great favour from the Queen Mother.

Line 3 (yin): Your promotion is approved by all. The causes of regret are gone.

Line 4 (yang): You are promoted, yet you have to hide like a rat. This portends danger.

Line 5 (yin): The causes of regret are gone. You no longer need to worry about the results. Proceed, it will be auspicious. There will be no misfortune.

Line 6 (yang): You have already advanced to the extreme corner. Your heart is tied down by someone. If you launch an expedition, there will be danger, though you will emerge fine and unharmed. This portends difficulty.

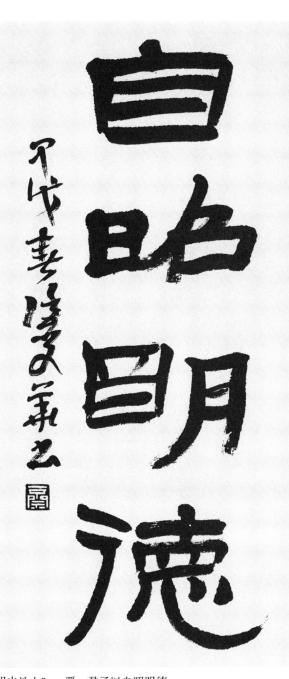

35《象》曰：“明出地上”，晋。君子以自昭明德。

Jin is a sign of Brightness rising over the Earth. In observing the sign, the superior man will let his illustrious virtue shine upon the world.

The Interpretation

The Time will come when one's contribution is recognized by people at the top. Yet before the Sun emerges, it will be blocked by mountains and clouds.

Thanks to your good work, your company has survived a major crisis and begins to prosper. The board of directors has decided to give you a special raise and often seek your advice. Yet your colleagues fail to appreciate your contribution. Some may even suspect that favouritism is the very key to your success. They may all be dubious of you and avoid you all together. Keep a low profile. For the Time being, do not try to reach out to people, for your friendly gestures will only push them further away. Let your good work prove to them your ability. The Time will come when they accept your leadership. With their support thus won, you may proceed with your plans of expanding the business.

The Hexagram indicates that you may encounter problems in your personal relationship the moment you climb to the apex. Your loved one begins to complain that you are always not by his/her side. You begin to wonder whether you should spend more time with him/her. Yours is a difficult decision to make.

Prioritize your activities. Then you will find the precious time with your loved one.

The Sun will rise high in the sky. Let the Sunshine reach every corner of your world.

Hexagram 36   Ming Yi—Darkening of the Light

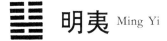 明夷 Ming Yi

The Symbols
Outer Earth
Inner Fire/Sun

The Judgement
If you are asking about the difficulty you are facing, this portends good fortune.

The Conditions
Line 1 (yang): The crying pelican (*ming yi*)[50] is flying, its wings drooping. The superior man is travelling. He has not eaten anything for three days. He has a long way to cover, and the lord has reprimanded him.

Line 2 (yin): The crying pelican is wounded in the left thigh. The superior man [is wounded but] is saved because his horse is strong. Good fortune.

Line 3 (yang): The crying pelican is flying over the south hunting ground. The superior man has captured a big animal. If you are inquiring about an illness, this portends of no good fortune.

Line 4 (yin): The superior man enters the left chamber. He gets the message of the Hexagram "Ming Yi", and leaves the mansion.

Line 5 (yin): Like the wise man Jizi,[51] the superior man understands the philosophy behind the Hexagram "Ming Yi". This portends good fortune.

Line 6 (yin): There is no light; it is dark. The pelican at first soars high in the sky, but then alights on the ground.

36《象》曰：明入地中，明夷。君子以莅众用晦而明。

Ming Yi is a sign of Brightness sinking into the Earth. In observing the sign, the superior man veils his brightness, though his virtue still shines.

The Interpretation

The Sun has set, and the world darkens. No one will be able to arrest the setting of the Sun. And burning oneself out will not light up the Hades.

The whole organization you are working for is rampant with corruption and hypocrisy, and people at the top are the very sources of the evil practices. Men of integrity and high calibre have tried to correct the situation. They admonished the leader, endangering their career and honour. And they end up disgraced. You consider quitting. Yet you are devoted to the mission of the organization. Out of the organization, you can find no other way to realize your ideal. So you have the urge to do something to repair the situation.

Yet the Hexagram portends of the prevalence of the forces of darkness. Do not endanger yourself. Dim your Brilliance, but maintain your integrity. Preserve your Position, and hopefully when there is a change of leadership or when the people at the top come to their senses, you will still be there, and help.

An allusion to the historical figure Jizi, this Hexagram speaks particularly to statesmen in a corrupted country.

When the sky Darkens, let the Pelican alight on the ground so that it may soar high in the Day.

Hexagram 37 Jia Ren—The Family

 家人 Jia Ren

The Symbols
Outer Wind/Influence
Inner Fire/Virtue[52]

The Judgement
If you are asking about a female member of your family, this portends good fortune.

The Conditions
Line 1 (yang): You have prohibited improper behaviours in the family. The causes of regret are gone.
Line 2 (yin): She has made no mistakes.[53] She devotes herself to household duties like cooking. An auspicious portent.
Line 3 (yang): You are stern with your family. There may be occasions when you regret your harshness. Yet things will turn out well. If your womenfolk and children frolic about and romp around all day long, the family will be disgraced in the end.
Line 4 (yin): A wealthy family. Highly auspicious.
Line 5 (yang): Like a king, you will have a large family.[54] There is nothing for you to worry about. Auspicious.
Line 6 (yang): Honourable and respectful, you will enjoy good fortune in the end.

The Interpretation
One may be a successful businessman, or a respected community leader. Yet there are times when one may not be sure whether he can claim success in handling family affairs.

If you are wondering what your wife and children are doing

37 《象》曰：风自火出，家人。君子以言有物而行有恒.

Jia Ren is a sign of Wind blowing forth from Fire. In observing the sign, the superior man will have substance in his words and consistency in his good deeds.

while you are busy working all day long, this Hexagram portends good fortune. At times, they complain that you are too stern with them, treating them like your subordinates. Reflect, and show them the affection of a husband and father, yet do not let affection interfere with proper discipline. Kids will bend to peer pressure like grass to Wind. If you do not exert Influence on the child, his peers will. So be sure to check in time any unhealthy outside Influence. If unchecked, minor problems will soon snowball into a major crisis in the family.

With the house thus kept in good order, you will have pride in a society where most people believe that he who cannot rule his family cannot be entrusted with the ruling of a state.

Let the Fire in you light the Fire of Virtue in your child. Let the Wind of your Influence blow strongly against the Wind of outside Influence when the Fire is still flickering.

Hexagram 38 Kui—Parting

 睽 Kui

The Symbols
Outer Fire
Inner Swamp

The Judgement
This portends good fortune only for trivial matters.

The Conditions
Line 1 (yang): There is no need to regret. Nor do you need to run after the stray horse. It will come back. You will come across an ugly man, but there will be no harm.

Line 2 (yang): You will meet your lord on a narrow street. There will be no harm.

Line 3 (yin): You will see a wagon being hauled back, with a buffalo dragging it. The wagon driver is branded on the forehead, his nose cut off. He makes no progress in the beginning but he succeeds in the end.

Line 4 (yang): Your friends part company with you. You continue on your own. You will come across an important man. You are sincere with each other. Act prudently as if you are in danger, then there will be no harm.

Line 5 (yin): The causes of regret are gone. Your clansmen are having a feast. Go join them. There will be no harm.

Line 6 (yang): Your clansmen part company with you. You continue on your own. On the way, you see a pig, then a carriage full of strangely dressed people.[55] You are alerted and draw your bow, but then you lay your bow aside, for they are not robbers. They are a wedding procession. Go on with your way. It will

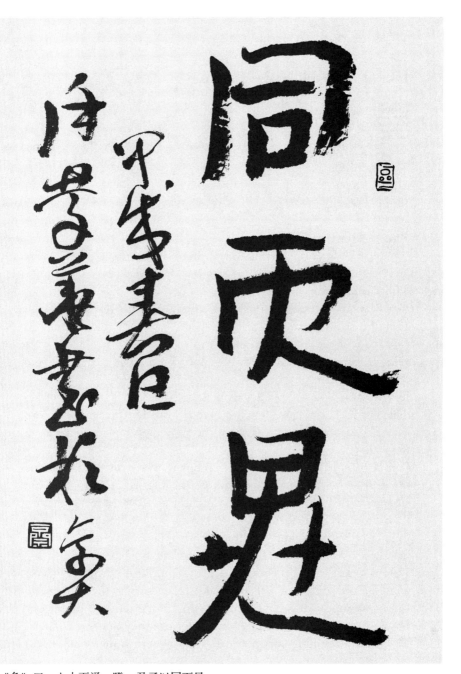

38 《象》曰：上火下泽，睽。君子以同而异。

Kui is a sign of Fire over a Swamp. In observing the sign, the superior man will find out where the similarity lies, and yet mark the differences.

rain, and there will be good fortune.

The Interpretation

We meet, we part, and we go our separate ways. Sad one may be, reluctant one may be, yet when the Time comes, one will have to say farewell, and go on an unfamiliar path, all alone. And on this new path, one will meet someone else. For in Meeting lies the seed of Parting, and in Parting, that of Meeting. Such is the Tao of relationships.

You have quarrelled with your boss, your friend, or your beloved one. If it was over a trivial matter that had grown out of proportion, this Hexagram portends reconciliation in the end. Yet if it was over a major difference, then you may have to be prepared to go on your own way. On this unknown path, expect to meet all kinds of strange people. Be sincere, and be on constant alert, then there will be no harm. When the Time comes, your paths will cross again.

To an entrepreneur, the Hexagram has this to say: your right-hand man will quit, and you will have hard time looking for a substitute. But relax, for the Hexagram indicates that unless you have hurt his pride, he will return in time. Meanwhile, you may need to find someone to fill his vacancy. Expect to see all kinds of people applying for the job.

To someone who has just quitted, expect to come upon your former boss on an unexpected, and even embarrassing, occasion. Take heart, for the Hexagram indicates no harm. Though your quitting has caused much chaos, he will not react in malice.

The flames of the Fire leap up; the water of the Swamp flows down. The Time will come when two people of different temperaments move in different directions.

Hexagram 39 Jian—Obstacles

 蹇 Jian

The Symbols
Outer Water/Danger
Inner Mountain/Stop

The Judgement
There will be advantages in the west and south, but not in the east and north. Meeting a powerful man will bring good fortune. An auspicious portent.

The Conditions
Line 1 (yin): If you proceed, there will be obstacles. If you retreat, you will make a name.

Line 2 (yin): The king and his minister are in difficulty. They are constrained by the circumstances.[56]

Line 3 (yang): If you proceed, there will be obstacles. If you retreat, the situation will be reversed.

Line 4 (yin): If you proceed, there will be obstacles. If you retreat, you will find your ally.

Line 5 (yang): You will face a major obstacle. But then you will win a fortune.

Line 6 (yin): If you proceed, there will be obstacles. If you retreat, you will have great achievement. You will have advantages meeting the powerful man.

The Interpretation
To many a thinker, courage and determination are the keys to deal with Obstacles. Yet to the author of *Changes*, keeping in tune with Time is the only wise move. Danger and Opportunity

39 《象》曰：山上有水，蹇。君子以反身修德。

Jian is a sign of Water on top of a Mountain. In observing the sign, the superior man will examine himself, and cultivate his own virtue.

are twins, and only if one is in sync with Time can he tell the one from the other. If one fails to understand Time and mistakes Danger for Opportunity, one will end up forcing his way on in the wrong direction.

You have accumulated enough capital, and over the years, have established your own network of business relations. You believe that the Opportune Time has come for you to leave the company and start a business of your own. Yet your boss and your comrade-in-arms are in dire straits, and you are the only one who can reverse the situation. But staying behind would mean you have to give up your own Opportunity. So you want to forsake them and proceed with your own plan.

Yet the Hexagram forecasts of a different scene: if you proceed, you will encounter Obstacles. But if you stay behind, you will win the admiration of all in a society where people at the Time value loyalty. Your Opportunity, the Hexagram indicates, lies not in your new venture, but in the Danger your company is facing. Retreat to lead your comrades out of difficulty. Then you will have fame. Then you will achieve what you have not dreamed of.

Stride forward, and you will plunge into an abyss. Retreat, and you will have a Mountain of fame and success to sit on top of.

Hexagram 40 Jie—Removing Obstacles

 解 Jie

The Symbols
Outer Thunder/Action
Inner Water/Danger

The Judgement
There will be advantages in the west and south. If you do not have a clear plan, it will be more auspicious to return. If you do have a plan, then the earlier you go, the better.

The Conditions
Line 1 (yin): No misfortune.
Line 2 (yang): You catch three foxes in a hunting, and find three bronze arrow heads. This portends good fortune.
Line 3 (yin): You carry a burden on your back while riding on a carriage. This will draw the attention of robbers. A sign of danger.
Line 4 (yang): Unfasten yourself, and quicken your pace. When the money arrives, people will have confidence in you.[57]
Line 5 (yin): The superior man's problems are solved. Auspicious. He has won the confidence of others.
Line 6 (yin): The noble man shoots at a hawk on a high wall. He gets it. No misfortune.

The Interpretation
The Chinese term for Crisis is *wei ji,* literally "Danger and Opportunity". Herein lies a major precept in the *Changes*: Danger and Opportunity always go hand in hand. If Danger is in sight, Opportunity will soon appear.

The market is full of Opportunities, though most people

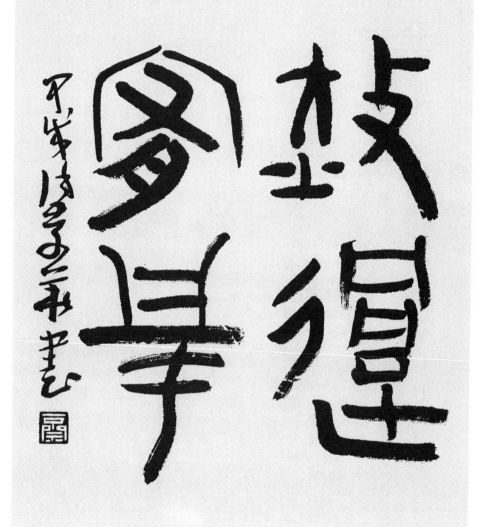

40 《象》曰：雷雨作，解。君子以赦过宥罪。

Jie is a sign of Thunder and Rain. In observing the sign, the superior man will pardon the offender and forgive the transgressor.

cry Danger. Your judgement is correct. Go ahead and increase your investment. You will have a minor gain initially. But to harvest a bigger return, you may have to borrow from the bank. The financial "difficulty" you are apparently in while you are increasing your investment will draw the attention of your competitors. They may want to strike you down at the time while you are most financially vulnerable. So keep an eye on their moves. Meanwhile, your business associates are watching, hesitating to go along with your plan. When the loan you have been waiting for arrives, you will reap huge profits. But here is a word of precaution: stride forward only if you have a detailed plan and have a clear picture of the whole situation. For if Opportunity is there, Danger will be close by.

At the moment, you may have some problem in your personal relationship. You and your loved one may have to go through a period of Water and Fire.[58] But if the two of you can see through the smog, you will eventually walk hand in hand down the aisle in the Thunderous applause of friends and relatives.

Behind the stretch of Water and Fire lies a vast expanse of luxuriant forest. Action in prudence will lead you to the world of Opportunity.

Hexagram 41 Sun—Cutting Down

 损 Sun

The Symbols
Outer Mountain
Inner Swamp

The Judgement
If you are sincere, this is highly auspicious. There will be no harm. What you portend about is fine. It will be advantageous to go ahead. Two large bowls of grain will be enough for the sacrifice.

The Conditions
Line 1 (yang): With reverence, attend the sacrificial activities.[59] Then there will be no harm. You may, as far as it is appropriate, cut down on the money presented for use in the sacrifices.
Line 2 (yang): This portends good fortune. But if you launch an expedition, there will be danger. Not only will you fail to cut down on the influence of your adversary but you also will add to his strength.
Line 3 (yin): When three people journey together, one will be diminished. When one person travels alone, he will meet a new friend.
Line 4 (yin): If you seek to be cured of your illness, be sincere in the sacrifices. Then you will have reasons to be happy. No harm.
Line 5 (yin): You may add to your offer a tortoise worth ten strings of cash. They will not reject the offer. Highly auspicious.
Line 6 (yang): Do not cut down on the offer. Add to it. Then there will be no harm. This portends good fortune. It will be advantageous to go on a long trip. You will obtain servants, though not a house of your own.

41《象》曰：山下有泽，损。君子以 惩忿窒欲.

Sun is a sign of a Swamp at the foot of a Mountain. In observing the sign, the superior man will subdue his anger and curb his desires.

The Interpretation

At any given moment, one's resources are limited. If one wants to Add to the expenses on a sector, he has to Cut Down on the expenses of the other. The guiding word in simple modern term is "prioritize". The *Book of Changes* speaks of four elements for one to consider before he decides on what to Add to, and what to Cut Down: one's own Ability and Resources, his Absolute Position, his Position relative to the Positions of different people in the scene, and the dominant forces of the Time.

There are too many social activities you have to take part in. You are exhausted, financially and physically, and yet you are wary that if you decline any invitation, you may ruin the good relation you have worked so hard to build up.

The Hexagram gives you this counsel: attend the functions, show your respect to the host, but Cut Down on the time and energy spent on the less important gatherings. People in a similar Position like yours will understand. And those in an inferior Position will appreciate your making the effort.

With your time and resources thus reserved, concentrate on the more important functions. Sacrifice the symbolic "tortoise" only to those who occupy a Position higher than, *and related to*, yours.

You may have hard time juggling between two prospective marriage partners. Make up your mind and settle down with one of them, for no three people can "journey together" for long. Otherwise, you will be the one who is dumped, and the two of them will each find his/her mate.

Dredge the Swamp, and add to the height of the Mountain.

140

Hexagram 42 Yi—Increase

 益 Yi

The Symbols
Outer Wind
Inner Thunder

The Judgement
It will be advantageous to go afar. It will be profitable to cross the Great Stream.

The Conditions
Line 1 (yang): It will be advantageous to launch a big project. Highly auspicious. No misfortune.
Line 2 (yin): You may add to your offer a tortoise worth ten-strings of cash. The offer will not be rejected. This will bring good fortune in the long run. The king will make sacrifice to God. Auspicious.
Line 3 (yin): Add to your offer in the case of a funeral. No misfortune. Be sincere, and walk in the way of the Mean. Holding the jade tablet denoting your rank, report to the lord.[60]
Line 4 (yin): Walk in the way of the Mean. Report to the lord, and he will follow your advice. He will use and rely on you in important matters, such as the removing of the capital.
Line 5 (yang): Be sincere and grateful. Don't query the lord. Highly auspicious. Be sincere and be thankful for the favour bestowed on you.
Line 6 (yang): You don't know whether to add to it, or to attack it. You are undecided. A bad sign.

The Interpretation
When people talk of investment, they often tend to think

141

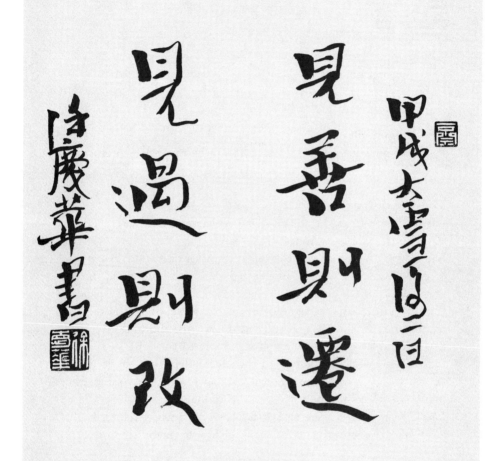

42《象》曰：风雷，益。君子以见善则迁，有过则改。

Yi is a sign of Wind and Thunder. In observing the sign, the superior man will, when he sees good, imitate it; and if he has faults, will rid himself of them.

in terms of the flow of cash. Yet there is a more sophisticated kind of investment—in the realm of human hearts.

You think you have identified the most important one with whom you want to establish a good relation. But the Hexagram asks you to think twice before committing yourself to this relationship. And once you have identified your "lord", remain faithful to him, or you will be despised by all. Present to him your symbolic "tortoise", but do not expect any immediate favour in return. Offer your advice when he is in power. When he is in need, Increase your offer of help. But always bear in mind your Position in relation to His. Do not, even in offering help, trespass the subtle line of distinction. Follow always the Doctrine of the Mean. If you are sincere, truthful and dutiful, your lord will appreciate your effort. But he will show his appreciation at his own pace, and in his own way, and not necessarily in the way you expect. Be grateful. Do not grudge. You will have nothing to gain by attacking your lord, for even before the battle is joined, you are already defeated, in the field of human hearts.

For those seeking advice on a marriage relationship, the lord the Hexagram refers to is your prospective partner. Increase your "investment" in your chosen one. But do not trespass the line.

The Thunder roars. The Wind howls. And the two will Add to each other's power.

Hexagram 43 Guai—The Decisive

 夬 Guai

The Symbols
Outer Swamp/Water
Inner Heaven/Cloud

The Judgement
Evil men have climbed to the top positions at the king's court. With sincerity, cry aloud and alert people to the danger. Alert your own people first. But do not launch an attack yet. It is advantageous to have a long-term plan.

The Conditions
Line 1 (yang): You are strong, yet you occupy a Position as low as that of the front toe. If you go ahead rashly, you will not win. Misfortune.

Line 2 (yang): You have cried the alarm. Even if you are attacked at night, you don't need to worry.

Line 3 (yang): You are strong, and occupy a Position where your facial expression will be observed by all. This is dangerous. The superior man decisively pushes on his way alone in the rain. He is soaked and shows signs of anger. No misfortune.

Line 4 (yang): There is no skin on your thighs. So you walk slowly and unsteadily. If you act together with others like a sheep following its companion, there will be no regrets. Yet you would not believe in these words.

Line 5 (yang): A goat bouncing along the middle way. No misfortune.

Line 6 (yin): You failed to cry the alarm in time. There will be danger in the end.

43 《象》曰：泽上于天，夬。君子以施禄及下，居德则忌。

Guai is a sign of Water surging up Skyward. In observing the sign, the superior man will share his riches with his subordinates and refrain from claiming all the merits.

The Interpretation

Many people tend to believe that a Decisive man working for a just cause will eventually win. Yet the author of *Changes* has this to add: he will eventually win, only if he is not already destroyed in the first place by his failure to take into account his varying Position at the ever-changing Time. In the event of misjudgement of Position and Time, the more Decisive one is, the more disastrous his defeat will be.

The Hexagram speaks to statesmen, community leaders and entrepreneurs. Your party/organization is occupied by evil people at the top. You are filled with righteous anger. A Decisive man of strong will, you want to rid the party/ organization of the evil influences. Yet the Hexagram cautions you: consider your Position. You will act in vain if your Position is as low as that of a toe. If you are in an estimable but yet not powerful enough Position, you must act with extra prudence, for yours is a more dangerous Position. Do not show your anger. Do not act alone. Rally people of your kind around you. Awaken them to the Danger the organization is facing. Once you have built up your influence and rightfully occupied the Position of the sovereign, you will win, even if you act like "a goat bouncing along the middle way".

The cleansing Rain will come in torrents when enough Clouds have accumulated.

Hexagram 44 Gou—Encountering

 姤 Gou

The Symbols
Outer Heaven/Sky
Inner Wind

The Judgement
If the girl is too strong for you, don't marry her.

The Conditions
Line 1 (yin): She is tied to the bronze handle of the distaff. A good portent. If her tie is loosened and she runs all about, there will be misfortune. She will then be like a pig jumping all about, looking for her mate.[61]

Line 2 (yang): The fish is in the kitchen.[62] No harm. Do not serve the guests with it.

Line 3 (yang): There is no skin on your thighs. So you walk slowly and unsteadily. Despite difficulties, there will be no major harm.

Line 4 (yang): The fish is not in the kitchen. This will give rise to quarrels. Misfortune.

Line 5 (yang): Wrap the gourd with medlar tree leaves—this looks good. But if the gourd falls and smashes, it is only natural.[63]

Line 6 (yang): The knocking of horns[64]—this portends difficulties. Yet there will be no misfortune.

The Interpretation
In this Hexagram, the only *yin* element lies at the first Position. This is a strong *yin* force that will boldly take the initiative to approach the five *yang* elements, though only the *yang* in the fourth line is its appropriate partner.

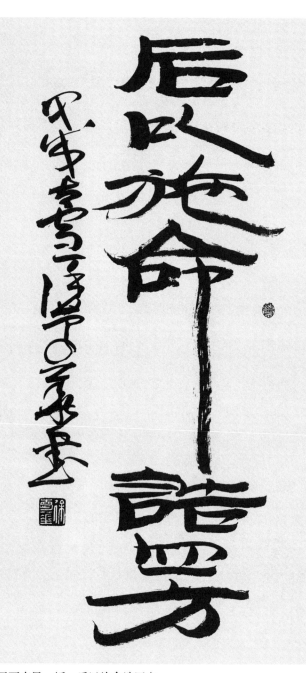

44《象》曰：天下有风，姤。后以施命诰四方。

Gou is a sign of Wind blowing under Heaven. In observing the sign, the sovereign will propagate his instructions to the four quarters of the world.

Apparently, this Hexagram refers to a marriage relationship. A man who gets this Hexagram must think twice before he decides to walk down the aisle. His prospective mate is a very strong and aggressive woman. If she has been well-disciplined by her parents and is willing to fulfil her wifely duties, there will not be much harm. If she is too "liberated" to care about wifely loyalty, one must have a second thought. If the man himself is charismatic enough to hold the woman's heart, it will also be fine, though the two will clash occasionally. Yet the marriage between a timid man and a strong-willed, unrestrained woman will soon fall and smash like the symbolic gourd; the marriage bond will not be able to secure it for long.

A woman who gets this Hexagram must take note of this: do not make your man feel threatened. Although in a modern society it is not improper for a woman to take the initiative, avoid giving him the impression that you will run after other men as you have approached him.

This *yin* element, as in many other cases, can also represent any supposedly passive person reaching all out for a business partner.

The gusty Wind rises Sky-high. Will it soften into a breeze and sail gently with the Cloud?

Hexagram 45 Cui—Gathering Together

 萃 Cui

The Symbols
Outer Swamp/Water
Inner Earth/Soil

The Judgement
Auspicious. The king will visit the ancestral temple. It will be advantageous to meet the powerful man. Success. This portends profit. Use a cow for the offering, then it will be auspicious. It will be profitable to proceed.

The Conditions
Line 1 (yin): If you are not entirely devoted, you will ruin your own hope of gathering together with the man of your heart. If he beckons you, go and hold his hand. Others may laugh at you. Don't bother about it. There will be no misfortune going to him.[65]
Line 2 (yin): Concentrate on the one, just like an archer pointing his arrow on his target. Then it will be auspicious. There will be no misfortune. With sincerity, your sacrifice will be accepted, though your offerings may be meagre.
Line 3 (yin): How one wants to gather together with her beloved! How sad one laments! This is not particularly auspicious, yet going to him will cause no misfortune. There will be some obstacles.
Line 4 (yang): Highly auspicious. No misfortune.
Line 5 (yang): You are in the Position to gather people together. No misfortune. You may not have the confidence of everyone, but this Line portends of good fortune in the long run. The causes of regret will soon be gone.
Line 6 (yin): Unable to find her mate, one sighs and weeps. No

45《象》曰：泽上于地，萃。君子以 除戎器，戒不虞。

Cui is a sign of Swamp water flooding over the Earth. In observing the sign, the superior man will have his weapons ready in order to guard against the unforeseen.

misfortune.

The Interpretation

When it comes to love, men can be very timid. And sometimes a woman has to guide her man. But this she has to do in the way of the *yin*—persistent, and yet receptive.

Devote your heart to the man you have chosen. *Wait* for him and him only to beckon you. When he does, do not let the traditional precepts of female demureness restrain you from responding, or your man will be discouraged. There may be gossips. Even though he is not certain of your devotion, when the Time comes, you will have the chance to show him that despite having many admirers, he is the only man you care. Then the causes of regret should be gone. Once he has faith in you, he will soon take you to the "ancestral temple" for the proper rites. However, if he is still suspicious despite your efforts, end the relationship. It is better for you to sigh and weep for the moment than to regret in the long run.

At the moment, your devotion to your company may be spoken of derisively as bootlicking. Your prompt action to carry out the instructions of your boss may be misinterpreted. Yet if you are loyal and sincere, you will eventually be accepted by all.

Moisten the Soil. And the flower will soon blossom.

Hexagram 46 Sheng—Ascending

 升 Sheng

The Symbols
Outer Earth
Inner Wind/Wood

The Judgement
Highly auspicious. It will be advantageous to meet the powerful man. No need to worry. It will be profitable to go south.

The Conditions
Line 1 (yin): You will ascend with the consent of all. Very auspicious.
Line 2 (yang): With sincerity, your sacrifice will be accepted, though your offerings may be meagre. No misfortune.
Line 3 (yang): You will ascend to a vacant town.
Line 4 (yin): The king will make offerings on the mountain in your territory.[66] Auspicious, no misfortune.
Line 5 (yin): An auspicious portent. You will ascend the stairs.
Line 6 (yin): Ascending at night—this portends good fortune for one who works diligently all day long.

The Interpretation
The ground is fertile. The climate is favourable. And the Time has come when the plant sprouts.

After all the years of hard work, your contribution is eventually recognized by all. Your loyalty, insignificant though it seems, is duly appreciated. You will be appointed to take charge of a new department, which the board of directors use to spearhead a new venture. In this new Position, you may have to undergo an

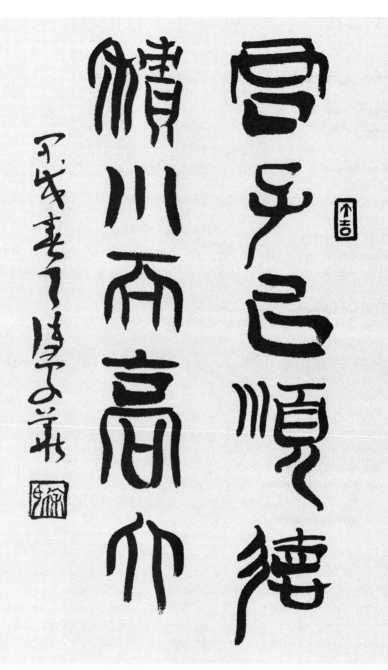

46《象》曰：地中生木，升。君子顺德，积小以高大。

Sheng is a sign of Wood underneath the Earth. In observing the sign, the superior man will abide by moral principles, for he realizes that small virtues accumulated will grow.

initial period of darkness when no one seems to be willing to offer help. Yet if you keep up with your good work, you will climb steadily up with the support of the people at the top. Eventually you will rise to enjoy a brighter day.

A diligent student who gets this Hexagram has reason to rejoice. All of your teachers speak in your favour, not just because of your diligence, but also because of a seemingly unimportant factor—the respect you show them all. The principal will choose you to represent the school in an important event or to take part in a special programme. They will hope to make you a model for other students. You will have to work extra hard, and with the support and encouragement of teachers and friends, you will survive the challenge and become a star of the school. Nevertheless, you may have to taste the bitterness of the jealousy of some of your peers.

The seed will soon break the ground. It will become a luxuriant tree.

Hexagram 47 Kun—In Plight

 Kun

The Symbols
Outer Swamp
Inner Water

The Judgement
Success. This portends good fortune for a superior man. No misfortune. Do not talk about your plight, for no one will believe you.

The Conditions
Line 1 (yin): One sits on a stump, feeling oppressed[67]—he has lost his way in a dark valley. For three years, he will see no other people.

Line 2 (yang): One is in want of food and drink. The noble one in crimson gown will come visit him. Offering sacrifices will bring good fortune. Going away will be disastrous. No misfortune.

Line 3 (yin): One's way is blocked by a rock, yet lying behind him is a forest of thorns and thistles. When he returns home, his wife is not to be found. Misfortune.

Line 4 (yang): Help comes slowly, for the driver has difficulty managing the golden carriage. Danger; yet help will eventually come.

Line 5 (yang): He is agitated,[68] for he finds the noble one in crimson gown oppressive. Relief will come very slowly. It will be advantageous to make offerings to the gods.

Line 6 (yin): He is entangled in creeping vines. He is agitated. He makes a move, and this causes regret. He is remorseful. It will be auspicious to go away.

47 《象》曰：泽无水，困。君子以致命遂志。
Kun is a sign of a Swamp without Water. In observing the sign, the superior man will devote himself to his life's ambition.

The Interpretation

For one time or another, every one of us may have to walk through a dark valley. This valley full of thistles and thorns will even seem to be the only world one has. Yet as soon as one recognizes that his is but a world of endless thistles and thorns, he will soon walk painfully away to a better new world.

Everyone is envious of your job. Yet you are the only one who knows what kind of pains and torments you have to suffer. You have to work day and night. And very often, when you drag your dead-tired body home, your disgruntled wife/husband is not there, for you have not had the time to water the flower of your marriage. And how many nights have you come home to her/him?

Despite your sacrifices, your boss is not appreciative. He always keeps a watchful eye on you and pretends to offer help when you are in trouble. But he will be conveniently tied up by something else. Help will only come after you have felt the pinch. No matter what you do, you are pricked. You can find relief only if you resort to flattery and "make offerings to the gods". You have considered quitting, yet you are wary for you are afraid to face the unknown future. But the Hexagram says: yours is only a dark valley of thistles and thorns. It will be better to go away and preserve your sanity and integrity.

If you are in a painful relationship, ask yourself this question: can the thorns and thistles be mowed? If not, you may consider ending the relationship.

The Water is drained, and the Swamp is dry.

Hexagram 48 Jing—The Well

 井 Jing

The Symbols
Outer Water
Inner Wind/Water-drawing Device[69]

The Judgement
The town is restructured, but the well remains at the same site. No gain, and no loss either. People come to draw water from the well, and then leave. [You, too, come to draw water.] Your jug has almost reached the water, but the rope is not long enough. In the end, the jug is broken. Misfortune.

The Conditions
Line 1 (yin): The well is muddy. No one drinks its water. Even birds will not come to this ruined well.
Line 2 (yang): You hate to find frogs at the bottom of the well.[70] Your jug is broken and leaks.
Line 3 (yang): You have cleaned out the well, yet no one comes to drink from it. You are sad, and you pray: may people draw from it. May the king be clear-minded. May all people benefit from it.
Line 4 (yin): The well is lined with bricks. No misfortune.
Line 5 (yang): The well is clear and limpid. The water is cold and clean. One may drink from it.
Line 6 (yin): After you have drawn from the well, do not cover it. Then people will believe you. Highly auspicious.

The Interpretation
Societies change. People change. And yet no society, and no people, should cast the past all away. There is always something

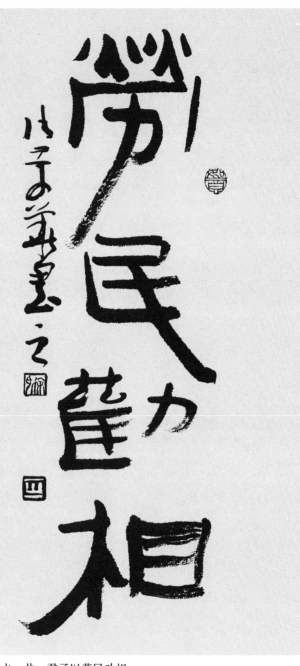

48《象》曰：木上有水，井。君子以劳民劝相。

Jing is a sign of Water spilling over a Wooden bucket. In observing the sign, the superior man will encourage the people to work hard, and exhort them to support one another.

vital that defines and binds a society, a people, or a relationship.

He who cherishes the good old family values, as well as one who prays that his/her spouse will taste with him/her the old-fashioned idea of love will find this Hexagram revealing. Teachers may also see this Well as the subject they teach.

This Hexagram is, however, specially pertinent to a scholar working to preserve and promote cultural heritage. At the moment, the picture is gloomy. You have tasted the nectar, and you want your people to share it. Yet no one seems to really care about their heritage. And those who want to drink from this Well find it ruined. And the water is muddy. Faked scholars and incompetent translators have so misinterpreted the classics that people cannot taste its sweetness. You hate to find these "frogs". Yet even your own "jug" is broken and leaks. There is really no good fortune. You are disappointed.

Take heart, for the Hexagram predicts that if you persist, you will succeed in repairing and cleaning the Well.

An entrepreneur who gets this Hexagram will soon find that people eventually agree to his judgement about the possible recovery of a declined sector of his company's business. Your "king" will be grateful once he has tasted the sweetness of the Well you have worked so laboriously to repair.

Repair the Well. Clean the Water. Design a new Water-drawing Device.

Hexagram 49 Ge—Reform

 革 Ge

The Symbols
Outer Fire
Inner Swamp/Water

The Judgement
You will win the confidence of the people when the day comes. Highly auspicious. This portends good fortune. The causes of regret are gone.

The Conditions
Line 1 (yang): Tie yourself up with the hide of a yellow cow [restrain yourself].

Line 2 (yin): When the day comes, reform it. You may proceed [when the day comes] and it will be auspicious. There will be no harm.

Line 3 (yang): Proceeding [before the Time comes] will be disastrous. This portends difficulty. Explain your ideas of reform to people again and again. Then you will win their confidence.

Line 4 (yang): The causes of regret are gone. You have won people's confidence and you can now go ahead with the reform. Auspicious.

Line 5 (yang): The powerful man reforms with the ferocity of a tiger. He has won the confidence of the people even before this divination is cast.

Line 6 (yin): The superior man makes changes erratically like a leopard. People's expressions change. Proceeding will be disastrous. Settle down, then this will portend good fortune.

49《象》曰：泽中有火，革。君子以治历明时.

Ge is a sign of a Fire in a Swamp. In observing the sign, the superior man will set the calendar in order and show people clearly the changes of time.

The Interpretation

Timeliness, a major concept of *Changes*, is the very key to successful Reform. If one lags behind Time, he will be cast aside. Yet if one runs ahead of Time, not only will his efforts be wasted, he may even put himself in jeopardy.

Corruption and evil practices are rampant. The country/system is too backward in many important aspects. You see the need to Reform. Yet for the moment, you have to restrain yourself. Wait, because the people are not awakened. Educate them, and make them see the light. When the Time comes, they will all see the need. Then and only then should you push forth your ambitious plan of Reform. When the Time comes, proceed in full vigour. Yet always float with the stream of Time. You may quicken the pace of the people, but you must not move in advance of them, or they will find your measures erratic. As the Taoist philosopher Zhuangzi advises: do what the Time calls for and allows, but not what you desire. You may help modify the Time, and yet you must always be in pace with Time.

If the strong Fire is not turned down in Time, the Water in the pot will soon all evaporate. If there is too much Water, the Fire will soon be put out by the boiling overflow.

Hexagram 50 Ding—The Tripod/Renewal

 鼎 Ding

The Symbols
Outer Fire
Inner Wind/Wood

The Judgement
Highly auspicious. Success.

The Conditions
Line 1 (yin): The Tripod is turned upside down, for one wants to pour the stagnant stuff out. A concubine's status is raised, for one treasures her son. No misfortune
Line 2 (yang): The food is in the Tripod. One's wife is jealous,[71] but she cannot get close to the Tripod. Auspicious.
Line 3 (yang): The carrying-rings of the Tripod are broken. One cannot move it. The fat flesh of the pheasant cannot be served. The wife cries like raining, for she regrets what she did. It will be auspicious in the end.
Line 4 (yang): A foot of the Tripod is broken. The Tripod overturns and the food prepared for the lord is spilled. Even the lord is soiled. Misfortune.
Line 5 (yin): The Tripod has bronze carrying-rings and a carrying-pole inlaid with gold. An auspicious portent.
Line 6 (yang): The Tripod has a carrying-pole inlaid with jade. Highly auspicious. No misfortune.

The Interpretation
The Wood has been accumulated. The Fire is ready. Are the three legs of the Tripod in good shape?

165

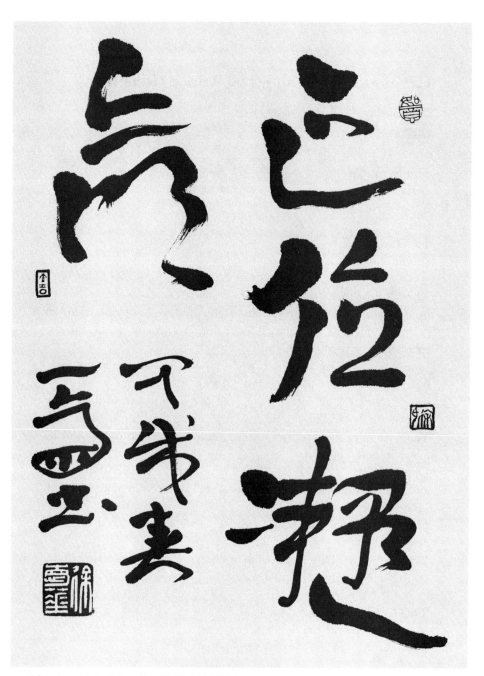

50 《象》曰: 木上有火, 鼎。君子以正位凝命。

Ding is a sign of Fire burning over Wood. In observing the sign, the superior man will keep to a correct position, so as to accomplish his mission.

You are ready to carry out your plans of Reform. You want to close a certain sector, and establish a new one. Yet you meet with opposition in this reshuffling. People who are afraid that they may lose out in this reshuffling are trying secretly to hinder your plans. Be lenient to those who have in the beginning boycotted the plan, for they did not understand. Explain to them that the old system is stagnant, and the country/organization needs the new system to inject new life into it. Assure them that they will not be cast aside, or they will spoil the plan, and you will be disgraced. Use them as the carrying-pole of the Tripod, and inlay the pole with gold and jade.

Those conducting a difficult negotiation should also reflect on this Tripod. One gives, one takes, and one compromises. Compromise may very well be the third leg your Tripod needs.

Know your Tripod.

Hexagram 51 Zhen—Thunder/Shock

 震 Zhen

The Symbols
Outer Thunder/Shock
Inner Thunder/Shocked

The Judgement
Success. The Thunder strikes, and you are shocked. But then you regain your composure, joking and chatting as usual. The roaring of the Thunder can be heard from a hundred miles away, startling everybody. And yet you remain calm; not a single drop of wine in your ladle is spilled.

The Conditions
Line 1 (yang): The Thunder strikes, and you are shocked. But then you regain your composure, joking and chatting as usual. Auspicious.

Line 2 (yin): The Thunder strikes with ferocity. You will suffer financial loss,[72] for you have climbed up mountain upon mountain. Don't be bothered by the loss, for you will recover in seven days.

Line 3 (yin): The Thunder strikes, and you are startled. Proceed despite the Thunder; there will be no harm.

Line 4 (yang): The Thunder strikes, and you are so startled that you fall down on the muddy ground.

Line 5 (yin): The Thunder strikes ferociously here and there. Yet you will not suffer loss; and you can continue to accomplish your task.

Line 6 (yin): The Thunder strikes, and wide-eyed, you move cautiously, watching every single step you make. This portends Danger. But the Thunder will not strike you. Your neighbour

51《象》曰: 洊雷, 震。君子以恐惧修省。

Zhen is a sign of roaring Thunders. In observing the sign, the superior man will be fearful of the wrath of Heaven. He examines himself and cultivates virtue.

will be the victim. Friends and relatives will spread gossip about you [before the dust settles].[73]

The Interpretation

Clouds have accumulated. A thunderstorm is approaching. Yet many an ordinary man will still be shocked by the Thunder.

There have been rumours that the authorities will take stern actions against malpractice in your field. Yet people do not seem to be prepared. You may also be perplexed by the severity of the measures. Stay calm, concentrate on dealing with the impending troubles instead of your fear. Since you are connected with so many people in your position, it is only natural that you will be a target of investigation when they are suspected. If you give in to fear and do something foolish, you will "fall down on the muddy ground". However, if you have been abiding by the rules, you will emerge unshattered. Your career will remain intact. You may, in fact, with the lesson you learnt in this storm, be more mature and will make great accomplishment in the future.

He who is Shocked by a Shock will be the victim of his own Shock.

Hexagram 52 Gen—Mountain/Steadiness

 艮 Gen

The Symbols
Outer Mountain/Steadiness
Inner Mountain/Steadiness[74]

The Judgement
You look steadily at her back; but you will not be able to see her front. You walk into her garden; but she is not to be found. No harm.

The Conditions
Line 1 (yin): Look steadily at her toes. No harm. This portends good fortune in the long run.
Line 2 (yin): Look steadily at her calves. You do not want to run after her for help, but you feel depressed.
Line 3 (yang): Look steadily at her girdle—it divides her upper body. Danger. Your heart will be burning with anxiety.
Line 4 (yin): Look steadily at her body. No misfortune.
Line 5 (yin): Look steadily at her cheeks. Organize your speech. The causes of regret are gone.
Line 6 (yang): Look steadily at her with sincerity. Auspicious.

The Interpretation
One may sometimes be awed by the loftiness of an ideal, just as one may be intimidated by the height of a mountain. Yet climbing steadily up, one will eventually come to the top.

You have an ambitious plan. Yet you have only a vague idea of how things will actually be like when the plan is realized. And you wonder whether you can realize such an ambitious project.

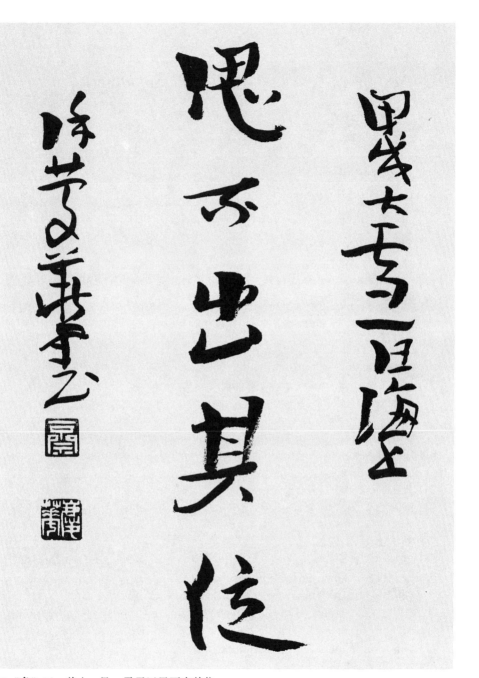

52《象》曰：兼山，艮。君子以思不出其位。

Gen is a sign of Mountain upon Mountain. In observing the sign, the superior man will not think of overstepping his authority.

Start from the beginning. Solve the problems step by step. With steady effort, you will be on the way to your destination. Yet there is always the danger that you, like so many people, will stop midway. Concentrate not on what you have already achieved. Look at the whole picture instead. Then you will know that you still have half of the way to go. Steadfastness and sincerity will take you steadily to the summit.

If you are inquiring about your chances with someone you like, the prospect looks good. But one precaution: do not be obsessed with "her/his girdle".

Steadiness comes with Steadiness.

Hexagram 53 Jian—Gradual Progress

 漸 Jian

The Symbols
Outer Wind/Tree
Inner Mountain

The Judgement
The marriage of a girl. Auspicious. This portends good fortune.

The Conditions
Line 1 (yin): A swan flies[75] to the shore. A young man is in danger, for there are criticisms of him. Yet there will be no harm.
Line 2 (yin): The swan flies to a large rock. He will enjoy his food and drink to his heart's content. Auspicious.
Line 3 (yang): The swan flies to the plains. The man on expedition will not return. The pregnant woman will not give birth. Danger. It will be advantageous to fight against the intruders.
Line 4 (yin): The swan flies to a tree. It finds a twig to rest on. No harm.
Line 5 (yang): The swan flies to the hilltop. Though the woman has no child for three years, she is not displaced by the concubines. Auspicious.
Line 6 (yang): The swan flies back to the plains. Its feathers can be used in the ceremonial dance. Auspicious.

The Interpretation
Though one may be highly capable and has the potential to make great progress, he will have to proceed gradually, for this is not the Time for a meteoric rise.

You are confident in yourself. With your talent and

53《象》曰：山上有木，漸。君子以居賢德善俗。

Jian is a sign of Wood growing on a Mountain. In observing the sign, the superior man will take up the role of propagating moral principles and improving the mores.

qualification, you are assigned to a Position that offers good prospect. Though this is only the first step of the ladder up, the special treatment you have received is already a target of criticism in a company where there are strict rules about promotion. Watch your steps. Self-satisfaction will entail danger. People may attack you. The projects you conceived may be sabotaged. And your men may be dismissed. Fight back, and you will be able to climb gradually to the top and stay there. For quite some time, no one can replace you. Meanwhile, you have to strive on so that your projects will bear fruit in time. Re-evaluate your own capability and the Time on every step up. You may consider taking a strategic retreat when the Time comes. Take up an honorary Position, so that you can still rest peacefully on your tree.

The prospect of your relationship also looks good. Despite some difficulties, the two of you will make it steadily to the aisle. And no one will be able to replace you. But it takes Time to develop the relationship.

One does not reach the Tree on top of the Mountain in one step.

Hexagram 54   Gui Mei—Marrying a Daughter Off

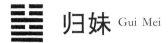 归妹 Gui Mei

The Symbols
Outer Thunder
Inner Swamp

The Judgement
This portends misfortune. No profits in the long run.

The Conditions
Line 1 (yang): One marries a daughter off, with her younger sister accompanying as the concubine. A lame man can still tread along. This portends good fortune.
Line 2 (yang): A one-eyed man can still see. This is a good portent for a solitary man.
Line 3 (yin): One marries a daughter off, with her elder sister accompanying as the concubine. But the younger one of the two is sent back.
Line 4 (yang): One marries off his daughter too late. Though late, the time will come when she will be married.
Line 5 (yin): The Lord Yi marries his daughter off. The bride's gown is not as pretty as that of her younger sister's. The moon is almost full. Auspicious.
Line 6 (yin): The girl carries a basket [in the wedding ceremony], but there is no fruit in it. The young man kills a sheep, but there is no blood. There will be no profit in the long run.

The Interpretation
All festive occasions are not blessings in the long run.
You have an idea to sell. And you have come up with a

54《象》曰：泽上有雷，归妹。君子以永终知敝。

Gui Mei is a sign of Thunder roaring above a Swamp. In observing the sign, the superior man will go through the whole process [of marriage], and he will know what the upside and downside [of a marriage life] are.

supporting plan. Your proposal will be accepted, though what people value in it is the supporting plan. For the moment, you may incline to call it a success. But the Hexagram indicates that the plan, since it is only partially implemented, will not bring any material gain to the company. So for you, this is not worth it in the long run.

Rethink your whole plan. Revise it where necessary. Do not be blinded by the rosy picture of your supporting plan. For only your main plan will bring long-term profits.

A man looking for a partner may take note of this: a lame man can still tread along. Do not marry someone you don't love for her wealth or her family's influence, or you will be tied down with an unhappy marriage; for it will not be so easy for you to send back the symbolic "wife" while keeping the "concubine".

Care for the Wife, not the Concubine.

Hexagram 55 Feng—Enlargement/Expansion

 Feng

The Symbols
Outer Thunder/Action
Inner Fire/Wisdom

The Judgement
Success. The king will come visit you. No need to worry. Carry out your activities at midday.

The Conditions
Line 1 (yang): You will meet your lord. Though you have ventured out for ten long days[76], there will be no harm. Proceed, for you will receive help.

Line 2 (yin): One joins his straw mats to make a mattress[77]. He sees the polar stars at midday. If you proceed, people will be suspicious. Yet if you are sincere, you may go ahead. Auspicious.

Line 3 (yang): One thickens the wadding of his mattress. He sees the small stars at midday. You will break your right arm [if you proceed], yet it is not a disaster.

Line 4 (yang): One joins his straw mats to make a mattress. He sees the polar stars at midday. You will meet your destined lord [so proceed]. Auspicious.

Line 5 (yin): Your potential is manifested. There are reasons for celebration. Auspicious.

Line 6 (yin): His empty mansion looks spacious. Its roof is covered with straw mats. If one peeps into it through the door cracks, one will see nobody. For three years, he is not to be seen. This portends danger.

55《象》曰：雷电皆至，丰。君子以折狱致刑.
Feng is a sign of Thunder and Lightning. In observing the sign, the superior man will pass his sentence, and carry out punishments.

The Interpretation

The ability to see what others do not see is rare. One may be misunderstood and suffers as a result. Yet with Wisdom as his guide, and Action his horse, one will find his way to wonderland.

The economy is doing extremely well. People are all basking in the sunshine. Yet you have observed some sign of regression. People may not believe you in the beginning, but if you are sincere, they will let you do what you think is necessary.

Carry out some measures to ensure that your company will still be shining when the night falls. Join the "mats" of the sector of business you believe will contain the polar stars. Thicken the "wadding of your mattress". When the night falls, you can lie down and enjoy the view.

You may encounter initial setbacks. But someone at the top will soon share your vision. He will lend you his hand. When the Time comes, you may be given the chance to manifest your ability. However, take care not to stretch the rules too far and do things that you are not in the Position to do. Otherwise, you will be out of the picture, leaving behind an "empty mansion".

In intimate relationships, your imagination will light up the candles of romance. Your partner will be amazed by the little, "silly" things you do. And these little "silly" things will form the "mattress" for the two of you to share your tender nights.

A student who has come up with a strange thesis will eventually be appreciated by a scholar who sees the ingenuity of the thesis. Elaborate your thesis. Collect more data, and broaden its application. With his guidance, you will make a name in the field.

At Midday, envision the scene when night falls.

Hexagram 56 Lü—Travelling

 旅 Lü

The Symbols
Outer Fire/Action
Inner Mountain/Non-action

The Judgement
Mild success. An auspicious portent for the traveller.

The Conditions
Line 1 (yin): The traveller is very fussy. This will get him into trouble.[78]
Line 2 (yin): He comes to an inn. With the money he carries with him, he buys a slave. An auspicious portent.
Line 3 (yang): The traveller's inn is on fire. His slave runs away. This portends danger.
Line 4 (yang): The traveller settles down in a hostel. He has made some profits, yet he is not contented.
Line 5 (yin): The traveller shoots a pheasant down with the first arrow. He wins the praise of everyone.
Line 6 (yang): The bird's nest is on fire. The traveller's laughter turns into tears. He loses his cow in the fields[79]. Danger.

The Interpretation
In Taoist parlance, Action means "going against the Natural flow of things"; and Non-action is "flowing with the Natural flow". Non-Action will be the path that a wise traveller takes.

You will make some fortune in an overseas investment. Make sure that you are not too meticulous about the minor details of your plans. Do not pick on your staff, or they will deflect. One

56 《象》曰：山上有火，旅．君子以明慎用刑，而不留狱．

Lü is a sign of Fire on a Mountain. In observing the sign, the superior man will strive to be judicious in imposing punishments. He will avoid protracting lawsuits.

good shot will win you fame and some material gains. Always remain in tune with Time. Give way when the Tide changes. Otherwise, you will be tied down to your overseas ventures while your business at home declines and you will not be able to find a "home" to return to.

You may be conducting a negotiation. You may come up with some new ideas that are not in the agenda. If you are not too fussy about the minor points, your proposal will be accepted. People may even admire the ingenuity of a particular important point you make. But do not go too far, or the whole proposal will be shelved. Let the natural flow of all forces dictate the negotiation.

The best move is the move that the Time wants you to make, not the move that *you* want to make.

Hexagram 57 Xun—The Yielding

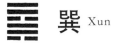 巽 Xun

The Symbols
Outer Wind/Yielding
Inner Wind/Yielding

The Judgement
Mild success. It will be profitable to proceed. It will be advantageous to meet the powerful man.

The Conditions
Line 1 (yin): One advances, then one yields. An auspicious portent for a man of valour.

Line 2 (yang): Yield, and retire to your couch. Let the shamans and witches perform the rituals. And what a commotion they will make! Auspicious. No misfortune.

Line 3 (yang): Yield, and yield again. There may be trouble.

Line 4 (yin): The causes of regret are gone. Your quarry will be plentiful.

Line 5 (yang): This portends good fortune. The causes of regret are gone. No disadvantages. Though there will be nothing to gain in the beginning, you will make a profit in the end. Act within seven days starting from the eighth day of this ten-day week to the fourth day of the next ten-day week.[80] Auspicious.

Line 6 (yang): Yield, and retire to your couch, or you may suffer a loss. This portends misfortune.

The Interpretation
He does not contend, therefore no one under Heaven can contend with him. So says Laozi.

57 《象》曰：随风，巽。君子以申命行事。

Xun is a sign of Winds. In observing the sign, the superior man will promulgate his orders, and carry out his plan.

Your proposal has been accepted, though people want to add to it some irrelevant points. They may want to spend quite some money on advertisement. They may want to invite the participation of some experts. Because of all these "modifications", your project will incur some loss initially. Yet yield to the opinion of the majority. Let them perform their "rituals", or you will meet with strong resistance. When the Time comes, they will let you take the stage. And you will make a star. When that Time comes, act swiftly, for the Time will not last long.

Your love will say yes to your proposal. Yet her parents and relatives will like a big wedding party. Yield to their wishes, or there may be trouble. The wedding gifts you will receive will cover most of your expenses. All these "rituals" are worthwhile, for yours will be a happy family.

A tree will be broken by a strong Wind. But the grass that bends to the Wind will survive the Wind.

Hexagram 58 Dui—Swamp/The Pleasing

 兑 Dui

The Symbols
Outer Swamp/The Pleasing
Inner Swamp/The Pleasing

The Judgement
Success. An auspicious portent.

The Conditions
Line 1 (yang): Be peaceful and pleasant. Auspicious.
Line 2 (yang): Be sincere and pleasant. Auspicious. The causes for regret are gone.
Line 3 (yin): Ingratiating to please others will bring misfortune.
Line 4 (yang): It will be a pleasant talk, though something remains unsettled. Those are just minor points. You have reasons to rejoice.
Line 5 (yang): Your counterpart has doubts over your sincerity. Danger.
Line 6 (yin): Take the lead and be pleasant.

The Interpretation
It takes two to make friends. But one must take the initiative.

You have identified someone whom you want to be your partner. If you are sincere and pleasant, the partnership will be fruitful for you and him. Though you may argue over something, your business relationship will not be affected. The only thing that can ruin a partnership is insincerity and distrust. If your partner is suspicious of your intentions sometimes, do not lose heart. Take the initiative to clear the misunderstanding. Always be pleasant, but not ingratiating, for ingratiating gestures are a

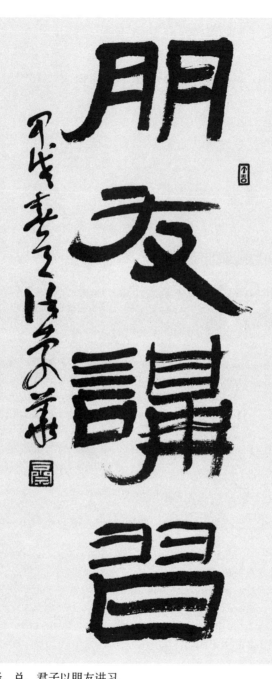

58《象》曰：丽泽，兑。君子以朋友讲习。

Dui is a sign of adjoining Swamps. In observing the sign, the superior man will join with his friends, and discuss matters with them.

major factor why one's partner may be dubious of his sincerity.

A young man or girl who gets this Hexagram is yearning for love. Be pleasant, but not ingratiating; positive and responsive, but not aggressive; or you will scare the other person away.

The Pleasing nourishes the Pleasing. The ingratiating repels.

Hexagram 59 Huan—Breaking Away[81]

 涣 Huan

The Symbols
Outer Wind/Wood/Boat
Inner Water/Stream

The Judgement
Success. The king will visit the ancestral temple. It will be advantageous to cross the Great Stream. An auspicious portent.

The Conditions
Line 1 (yin): It helps if one has the inner strength of a mare. Auspicious.

Line 2 (yang): He breaks away and escapes to his own threshold. The causes for regret are gone.

Line 3 (yin): He breaks himself away. No regrets.

Line 4 (yin): He breaks away from the crowd. Highly auspicious. He breaks away and retreats to a mountain. This is not what ordinary people will think of doing.

Line 5 (yang): He breaks away, and disseminates his great order. He breaks away, and thus the royal palace is free from danger.

Line 6 (yang): He breaks away from the bloody arena, and escapes to a distant land. No regrets.

The Interpretation
Emotionally, one may need to belong to a group. And when the Time comes, only a man of wisdom will have the strength to tear himself away.

You have been a member of your organization for a long time. But it is no longer the organization you first joined. The

192

59《象》曰：风行水上，涣。先王以享於帝，立庙。

Huan is a sign of Wind blowing over Water. In observing the sign, the ancient king made offerings to the Celestial Emperor, and set up an ancestral temple.

mission is distorted. The people struggle against one another for power, and increasingly you feel the pressure to join one faction or the other.

Keep sight of the reason why you joined the organization in the first place. Come home to your ideal. Do not, because of the emotional attachment, stay in it, or your very integrity will be at stake. Although people will not understand why you would give up the position in the organization, you yourself will know where your "royal palace" should be established. And as long as your "royal palace" remains intact, you may continue to disseminate your "great order".

Take the Boat, and cross the Great Stream.

Hexagram 60 Jie—Self-Restraint

 节 Jie

The Symbols
Outer Water
Inner Swamp

The Judgement
Success. Yet if you are tired of restraining yourself, then it will be impossible to tell what this portends.

The Conditions
Line 1 (yang): Do not venture out of the door. Then there will be no harm.
Line 2 (yang): If you do not venture out of the gate, there will be danger.
Line 3 (yin): If you cannot restrain yourself, you will have cause for lament. If you restrain yourself, there will be no harm.[82]
Line 4 (yin): If you can calmly restrain yourself, you will succeed.
Line 5 (yang): If you have joy in restraining yourself, it will be auspicious. Proceed, for help will come.
Line 6 (yin): If you are tired of restraining yourself, this portends danger. If you can restrain yourself, the causes of regret will be gone.[83]

The Interpretation
There is a Time to Act, and a Time to Restrain. Restraining oneself in the Time for Action will bring danger. Action in the Time of Restraint will incur harm. The first two lines of this Hexagram is a classic illustration of this concept of Time.

The Time calls for Restraint. Yet this does not mean one

60《象》曰：泽上有水，节。君子以制数度，议德行。

Jie is a sign of Water on a Swamp. In observing the sign, the superior man will set up the necessary systems, and examine the moral issues.

stops moving. One Restrains from pushing beyond the limit, yet one continues to push ahead. By such Actions in Restraint, you will accomplish your aim. Help will come to you if you have been Restraining yourself in all your moves. Never let success create the illusion that you can give free rein to your desires. If you are tired of Restraining, this otherwise auspicious portent may portends disaster.

At the moment, you are dangerously intimate with your boyfriend/girlfriend. Restrain yourself, or you may have regrets. Eventually, the two of you will be happily together. But failure to Restrain yourself at the present stage will ruin the relationship.

The Swamp will be flooded if Water pours down incessantly.

Hexagram 61 Zhong Fu—Sincerity/Faithfulness

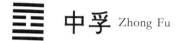 中孚 Zhong Fu

The Symbols
Outer Wind
Inner Swamp

The Judgement
Use a pig and a fish for the offering. Auspicious. It will be
advantageous to cross the Great Stream. This portends good
fortune.

The Conditions
Line 1 (yang): Be faithful, then it will be auspicious. If you have a
second one in your heart, then you will have no peace.
Line 2 (yang): A crane calls in the shade. Its mate answers. One has
some good wine. One wants to share it with his love.
Line 3 (yin): One encounters his rival. Now he beats the drum,
and now he retreats. Now he weeps, and now he chants.
Line 4 (yin): The moon is almost full. One's horse disappears. No
harm.
Line 5 (yang): They are sincere. They hold each other's hands
tight. No harm.
Line 6 (yang): The cock's crow reaches the sky. This portends
danger.

The Interpretation
Faithfulness is the cornerstone of every relationship. It is
also the anchor that secures one's heart in the sea of greed and
desires.

You are in an intimate relationship. But then someone else

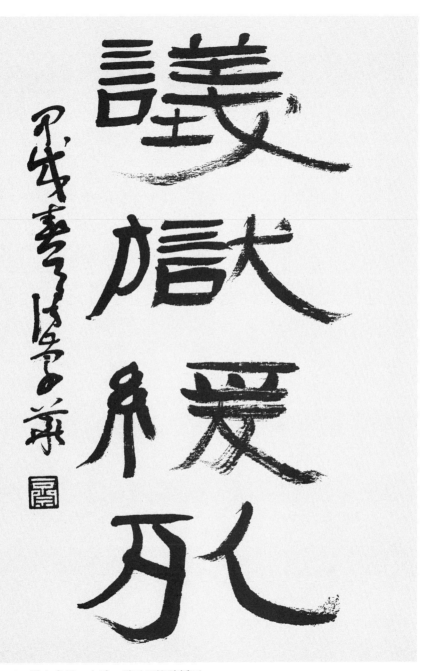

61《象》曰：泽上有风，中孚。君子以议狱缓死。

Zhong Fu is a sign of Wind blowing over a Swamp. In observing the sign, the superior man will examine criminal cases, and put off carrying out capital punishments.

appears in the picture. You are angry, and you are doubtful. Do not give up hope. Have faith in him/her. And most importantly, remain faithful. When "the moon is almost full", he/she will come and disappear with you riding your horse.

At the moment, someone is seeking your partnership in a new project. Yet you are not quite decided. Make up your mind soon, and be faithful to the chosen partner. On his part, he may have another one in his mind too. But the Hexagram portends that the two of you will eventually choose each other. Hand in hand, you will be able to "cross the Great Stream". But do this before the "cock crows", for when a new day dawns, the situation will be different.

As surely as the Wind ripples the water of the Swamp, Faithfulness of the one draws Faithfulness of the other.

Hexagram 62 Xiao Guo—Minor Mistakes

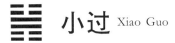 小过 Xiao Guo

The Symbols
Outer Thunder
Inner Mountain

The Judgement
Success. An auspicious portent. If this concerns small things, it will be fine. For great things, the prospect does not look good. The bird flies by, and its crying sound lingers on. Do not fly up, stay down below. Then it will be highly auspicious.

The Conditions
Line 1 (yin): The bird flies up, and thus incurs danger.

Line 2 (yin): You may find fault with your grandfather, though you should praise your grandmother. Do not extend your criticism to your lord, though you may praise his followers. No harm.

Line 3 (yang): Do not find fault with him, but try to prevent any future mistake. To let him have his way is to kill him. Danger.

Line 4 (yang): If he has made no mistake, do not find fault with him. Praise him instead. Take precaution against the impending danger. Do not ask for a portent concerning the distant future.

Line 5 (yin): Dense clouds have accumulated over the western suburb. The lord shoots. He gets his prey in its den.

Line 6 (yin): He who never praises but always criticizes is like a bird that flies up and incurs danger[84]. A dangerous sign. One may even say this will be disastrous.

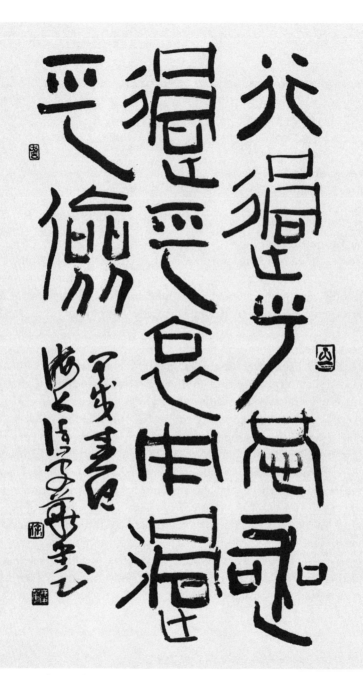

62《象》曰：山上有雷，小过。君子行过乎恭，丧过乎哀，用过乎俭。

Xiao Guo is a sign of Thunder roaring over a Mountain. In observing the sign, the superior man comes to realize that in showing respects, it is improper to be obsequious; in mourning, too grievous and in expenditure, too thrifty.

The Interpretation

One cares, thus one criticizes. Yet criticism without praise will draw the knives out on both sides. The one who criticizes and the one criticized will both be hurt.

You are observant and discerning. You can see that something has gone wrong while others are oblivious to the errors. Yet before you make any comments, weigh your words, weigh the possible consequence, and above all, weigh the importance of the matter to your listener.

If it is just a minor mistake, you may want to ignore it. If you have to point it out, try to find some good points in the way the other person is handling it. Soften your criticism with praises. However, if the matter is of major importance to the listener, you will have to be extra careful with your words. The Hexagram indicates that the listener cannot bear with any criticism about a matter vital to him. In this case, you may want to remain silent. Keep a low profile. Or you will be shot down like the bird that flies up.

For parents, this Hexagram has this to say: do not be too picky with your child. Yet do not pamper him. Do your best to prevent any unruly behaviour, but do not criticize without a good reason. Praise works better to lead the child to the proper path. Guide him step by step. Do not put him on the mountain of your "great expectations" and strike him down with the Thunder of your constant criticism.

One does not stand up on top of a barren Mountain when the Thunder roars.

Hexagram 63 Ji Ji—After Crossing/ Mission Accomplished

 既济 Ji ji

The Symbols
Outer Water
Inner Fire

The Judgement
Success. This portends of minor fortune. It will be auspicious in the beginning, but disorders will rise in the end.

The Conditions
Line 1 (yang): She has lifted her tassel, yet the ornamental tail of her skirt is wet[85]. No danger.
Line 2 (yin): She has lost scarf. There is no need to look for the lost item. It will be returned in seven days.
Line 3 (yang): King Gaozong attacked the Guifang, and he subdued it after three years. This line is not for the use of ordinary men.
Line 4 (yin): The lady's clothes are all wet[86]. She is on constant alert.
Line 5 (yang): The neighbour in the east slaughters an ox for his offering, but this is not as good as the sacrifice that the neighbour in the west offers [in sincerity]. The latter will enjoy great blessings.
Line 6 (yin): She is wet from top to toe. Danger.

The Interpretation
A mission has been accomplished. Yet how many people will look back and re-evaluate the situation before they embark on a new project?

You got a project off the ground. Yet do not, because of this

63《象》曰：水在火上，既济。君子以思患而预防之。

Ji Ji is a sign of Water boiling over Fire. In observing the sign, the superior man will think of potential dangers, and take the necessary precautions.

apparent success, have unrealistic expectations. Ask yourself how much resources you have already put in, and how much resources you still need to deal with unforeseen problems. Though your devotion will be appreciated, if you have immersed yourself entirely in it, you may be drowned when unanticipated troubles arise. Be on constant alert, then you may safeguard what you have already achieved.

In personal relationship, you have already won the other person's heart. But keep you head. There may be flaws in his/her character. Ask yourself seriously and honestly whether you can bear with those flaws in the days to come.

The Water is already boiling. Turn the Fire down.

Hexagram 64 Wei Ji—Before Crossing/Mission to be Accomplished

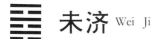 未济 Wei Ji

The Symbols
Outer Fire
Inner Water

The Judgement
Success. The little fox is going to cross the Stream. It will wet its tail. No long-term profit.

The Conditions
Line 1 (yin): It has wet its tail. Difficulties ahead.
Line 2 (yang): She lifts her tassel. This portends good fortune.
Line 3 (yin): Before the actual crossing, the sign has portended danger. Yet the Time has come for crossing, and it will be advantageous to cross the Great Stream.
Line 4 (yang): This portends good fortune. The causes of regret are gone, as in the case of a certain Zhen. He assisted King Gaozong to attack the Guifang[87]. They won after three years. And Zhen was lavishly rewarded by the great king.
Line 5 (yin): This portends good fortune. The superior man will have glory. He will be trusted. Auspicious.
Line 6 (yang): He is trusted, and he drinks to his success. No harm. He is drunk and his head all wet. Though he is trusted, his behaviour is not appropriate.

The Interpretation
   That the Hexagram "Before Crossing" should be preceded by "After Crossing" is an illustration of the philosophy of *Changes:*

64《象》曰：火在水上，未济。君子以慎辨物居方。

Wei Ji is a sign of Fire burning above Water. In observing the sign, the superior man will differentiate the nature of things, and place himself in a proper position.

the end of a stage of development marks the beginning of another. One should look back. But more importantly, one should look ahead, and be on constant alert.

You have accomplished a mission and are going to embark on a new one. Learn from your experience, but do not be bound by it. Take precautions against any problems you can foresee. Your experience helps but you must remain open to new approaches to dealing with the ever-changing situation. Then you have a good chance of success. Yet while you are enjoying the fruit of your success, always maintain a sense of danger. The moment you lower your guard, people will find fault with you. The moment you call it an end, the moment it will become new.

The Hexagram indicates that you have the tendency to indulge yourself when success is in sight. And it is because of this very tendency that the Hexagram portends that there will be no long-term profit.

Before Crossing, gauge the depth of the Water. Before Crossing, make sure you will not land on Fire.

One has crossed a Great Stream. Yet one still have a Great Stream to cross. One remains always at this constantly emerging juncture: Before Crossing.

Footnotes

1.   "Fortune" is a translation of *peng* 朋, which traditional scholars understand as "friends". My interpretation is based on Jin Jicang, *Zhouyi guaci xiangjie* (Taiyuan: Shanxi Gaoxiao Lianhe Chubanshe, 1993), p. 16.

2.   Many scholars interpret *xinan* 西 南 as "Southwest" and *dongbei* 东 北 as "Northeast". I follow Yang Ciguang's exegesis here. See Sun Guozhong and Dong Guanghe, eds. *Yijing zhinan* (Beijing: Tunjie Chubanshe, 1992), p. 221.

3.   The Ming scholar Lai Zhide (1525-1604) notes that *kun* symbolizes the mixture of *yin* and *yang* qualities. Here, line 3, a *yang* position, is occupied by *yin* (see Lai Zhide, *Yijing jizhu* [Shanghai: Shanghai Shudian, 1993], 1:40a) and demonstrates the same symbolic significance. The word *zhang* 章 is thus interpreted as "mixture" or "shining pattern". I agree with Lai's interpretation and believe also that this line still refers to the mare. The mare belongs in the *yin* category, and yet it possesses inner strength, which is a *yang* quality. Therefore, it is a befitting symbol of this mixture of *yin* and *yang* qualities. Hence my translation.

4.   *Ke* 可 is understood as *chengxin* 称 心 (accords with one's wishes) here. See Xu Zihong, *Zhouyi quanyi* (Guiyang: Guizhou Renmin Chubanshe, 1992), p. 19.

5.   Lai Zhide understands this as a reference to a battle between the *yin* and the *yang* elements (see Lai Zhide, *Yijing jizhu,* 1: 42a). I prefer to take the mare mentioned in the Portent as a sustained image in the hexagram; hence the term "the mare" in my translation of the lines. Since the mare is a symbol of the *yin* while the dragon a symbol of the *yang,* I believe that my reading is not far off.

6.   I follow Xu Zihong's interpretation. See Xu Zihong, *Zhouyi quanyi,* p. 21.

7.   The word zi 字 is sometimes interpreted as "to bear a child".

8.   Some scholars read the word *lu* as "deer". I adopt the interpretation of Lai Zhide and Hui Dong and take it as a loan word for the homonym meaning "hill".

See Lai Zhide, 2:6a and Hui Dong, *Zhouyi shu* (Chengdu: Bashu Shushe, 1993), p. 14.

9.   *Meng* 蒙 is a sort of grass and its meaning is extended to refer to an innocent child. Traditional scholars are more prompt to take its extended meaning. But I prefer its original meaning and read it as a symbol instead. In fact, this image of the grass is sustained in the whole hexagram. The weeding of grass is a symbol of the education of the child. See also Xu Zihong, *Zhouyi quanyi*, p. 32.

10.   Here I read *xue* as *xu* 洫, with the water radical.

11.   According to Li Jingchi, *zhang* 丈 in *zhangren* 丈人 refers to the mace that a military leader holds (see Xu Zihong, *Zhouyi quanyi,* p. 46). Some scholars believe that in this line we see someone making a divination about the *zhangren* (see Jin Jicang, *Zhouyi guaci xiangjie*, pp. 29-30).

12.   *Zuo* 左, usually meaning "left", should be read as "retreat" in this context (see Lai Zhide, *Zhouyi jizhu*, 3:5b).

13.   I follow Wen Yiduo's 闻一多 reading of the term *zhiyan* 执言 (see Xu Zihong, *Zhouyi quanyi,* p. 50).

14.   Some traditional scholars interpret *yuan* 原 as "once again", which does not make very good sense in the context. I adopt Wu Xinchu's interpretation here (see Wu Xinchu, *Jianming Zhouyi Duben* [Guangzhou: Huanan Ligong Daxue Chubanshe, 1993], p. 37.

15.   The wording of the judgement of this line, with the exception of the word *zheng* 征 , is identical with that for line 1 of the next hexagram. I take it as a loan word for the homonym meaning "portend", which appears in line 1 of hexagram 12.

16.   If one follows Xu Zihong's interpretation of the terms *bao huang* 包荒 and *ping he* 冯河 (see Xu Zihong, *Zhouyi quanyi,* p. 68), this line may be rendered as "An empty gourd may yet be used as a buoy for crossing the river."

17.   For the interpretation of *peng* 朋 as "cash" and *zhong xing* 中行 as "in the middle of the way", see Wu Xinchu, *Jianming zhouyi duben,* p. 41. See also Xu Zihong, *Zhouyi quanyi,* p. 68.

18.   *Fu* 孚 is read as "return" here (Wu Xinchu, *Jianming zhouyi duben,* p. 41).

19.   Some scholars take *peng* 彭 as a loan word for the script meaning "a lame shaman". I adopt Lai Zhide's interpretation here (see Lai Zhide, *Zhouyi jizhu,* 4:13a).

20.   For a discussion of the meaning of the word *ming* 鸣 , see Wu Chuxin, *Jianming zhouyi duben,* p. 47.

21.   I adopt Sha Shaohai's reading of *hui* 扐 as "courageous" (see Sha Shaohai, *Yi gua qian shi* [Guiyang: Guizhou Renmin Chubanshe], p. 97).

22.   Sha Shaohai glosses *xu* 盱 as "sluggishness" (see Xu Zihong, *Zhouyi quanyi,* p. 95).

23.   I adopt Gao Heng's reading of the word *you* 由 here (see Xu Zihong, *Zhouyi quanyi,* p. 95).

24.   Jin Jicang has argued convincingly that *peng* means "shells", which is cash to the ancient Chinese (see Jin Jicang, *Zhouyi guaci xiangjie,* p. 16); hence my translation. For a discussion of the meaning of the expression *he zen,* see Lai Zhide, *Zhouyi jizhu,* 4:26a.

25.   There are two major interpretations of this hexagram. Most traditional scholars tend to consider this as a reference to a woman choosing her man. Modern scholars, however, believe that this is a reference to the handling of slaves. My translation is deliberately ambiguous so that it can refer to both.

26.   Traditional scholars gloss the term *gu* 蛊 as "decay, spoiled". However, the wordings of the lines do not support such a reading. I follow Sha Shaohai's interpretation here (see Sha Shaohai, *Yi gua qian shi,* p. 112).

27.   Gao Heng has observed that in the time when the *Book of Changes* was written, the Chinese divided a month into three ten-day weeks. The word *jia* 甲 in the judgement refers to the first day of a ten-day week. Literally, this phrase means "three days before the day of *jia*, and three days after the day of *jia*" (see Xu Zihong, *Zhouyi quanyi*, p. 102). See also Jin Jicang, *Zhouyi guaci xiangjie*, pp. 39-40.

28.   I follow Hui Dong's (1691-1758) suggestion and read *han* 咸 as *gan* 感 (see Hui Dong, *Zhouyi shu, p. 67).*

29.   *Han* 咸 is read as *xian* 諴 here (see Xu Zihong, *Zhouyi quanyi,* p. 109).

30.   "Heavy hand" translates the term *gan* 甘, which Xu Zihong glosses as *qian* 钳, literally "pincers" (see Xu Zihong, *Zhouyi quanyi*, p. 109).

31.   For the meaning of *mie* 灭 as "cover" or "blocking the view", see Wu Xinchu, *Jianming Zhouyi duben*, p. 53.

32.   As Sha Shaohai and Zhou Zhenfu have shown, this Hexagram is a vivid description of wedding activities. Young guy and girls, as well as older people, all adorn themselves and march cheerfully to the bride's. At the same time, the bride's family is busy decorating her house (see Sha Shaohai, *Yi gua qian shi*, p. 134; and Zhou Zhenfu, *Zhouyi yizhu* [Beijing: Zhonghua Shuju, 1991], p. 83).

33.   A number of scholars have suggested that *mie* 篾 should read *meng* 梦 [夢].   For an example, see Zhou Zhenfu, *Zhouyi yizhu*, p. 85.

34.   Gao Heng glosses the word *dun* 敦 as "investigate" (see Xu Zihong, *Zhouyi quanyi*, p. 136). I adopt his reading here since it corresponds to the "Small Symbolism".

35.   Both Lai Zhide and Hui Dong read 已 as 止; meaning "to stop" (see Lai Zhide, *Yijing jizhu*, 6:10a; Hui Dong, *Zhouyi shu*, p. 90). Some modern scholars read it as 祀, or "to make offerings to the gods".

36.   Here, I adopt Xu Zihong's reading of the word *fen* 蕡 (see Xu Zihong, *Zhouyi quanyi*, p. 146). Following Wu Xinchu, I read the word *ya* 牙 as a loan word

for 栫, a homophone meaning "pigpen" (see Wu Xinchu, *Jianming Zhouyi duben*, p. 59).

37.   For a discussion of the meaning of the phrase, see Xu Zihong, *Zhouyi quanyi*, p. 146.

38.   I do not see how Mountain at the top of Thunder comes to mean "providing nourishment". The modern annotators I have consulted fail to give an acceptable answer. But Lai Zhide speculates that in each of the two trigrams of Mountain and Thunder is a *yang* line. The Mountain trigram relies on its *yang* force while the Thunder "nourishes" itself on its own. Thus the Hexagram symbolizes "the proper way of providing nourishment" (see Lai Zhide, *Yijing jizhu*, 6:15b). The Qing scholar Hui Dong, citing Jing Fang of the Han dynasty, points out that lines 2, 3, 4 and 3, 4, 5 form two trigrams of the Earth, which provide nourishment to "the myriad things". Therefore, the Hexagram is used to symbolize the provision of nourishment (see Hui Dong, *Zhouyi shu*, p. 93). My interpretation draws its inspiration from Hui Dong.

39.   The interpretation of this line is quite problematic. I adopt Lai Zhide's reading here (see Lai Zhide, *Yijing jizhu*, 6:17b).

40.   Refer to note 38 above.

41.   *Er* 貳 is a corrupted form for *zi* 资 (see Xu Zihong, *Zhouyi quanyi*, p. 160).

42.   I have in mind the Taoist master Zhuangzi, who beat the pot and sang at the death of his wife. One may protest that Zhuangzi was latter than the *Book of Changes*. My defence is that Zhuangzi, in making up the anecdote about himself, was probably alluding to an ancient story.

43.   There are two completely different interpretations of this Hexagram. Modern scholars generally gloss *xian* 咸 as "hurt". Despite its apparent merits, the modern interpretation fails to explain how "hurting" one's toes, etc. can be related to marrying a girl referred to in the Judgement. My translation is based largely on the interpretation of traditional scholars. For a brief analysis of the two interpretations, see Zhou Zhenfu, *Zhouyi yizhu*, pp. 113-114.

44.　　Modern scholars like Xu Zihong and Wu Xinchu point out that the word *xian* should mean "hurt". Though such an interpretation makes good sound in the case of the individual lines, it fails to explain the significance of the symbols and how "hurting" can be related to marriage. I therefore opt for the traditional interpretation.

45.　　I base my translation on Lai Zhide's interpretation of the term *zhen heng* 振 恆 (see Lai Zhide, *Yijing jizhu*, 17:16a).

46.　　Here I follow Lai Zhide's suggestion and interpret *chu* 畜 as "to stop, to restrain" (see Lai Zhide, *Zhouyi jizhu*, 7:21a).

47.　　In the edition that Hui Dong uses, *fei* 肥 is written as *fei* 飞 (see Hui Dong, *Zhouyi shu, p.* 111). Sha Shaohai and Xu Zihong further suggest that *fei dun* 肥 遁 means "running far away and soaring high" (see Xu Zihong, *Zhouyi quanyi*, p. 181).

48.　　I adopt Lai Zhide's interpretation of the word *yi* 易 here (see Lai Zhide, *Zhouyi zhengyi*, 7:29a).

49.　　The term "Kang hou" 康 侯 is problematic. I choose to follow Lai Zhide's interpretation (see Lai Zhide, *Zhouyi zhu,* 7:30b). With occasional exceptions, the translation will adopt Lai Zhide's reading of this Hexagram in general.

50.　　Sha Shaohai points out that *ming yi* should be read as *ming yi* 鸣 鹈 , a homophone meaning "a crying pelican" (see Sha Shaohai, *Yilin qianshi*, p. 221). In fact, one may read the term *ming yi* in four out of the six lines as referring to the bird. But the symbol is that of a sun setting on the earth, and favours a literal reading of the term *ming yi* as "wounding/ darkening of the light". Apparently, the going down of the pelican is compared to the setting of the sun, both of the two being metaphors of the hiding away of the superior man.

51.　　Jizi was a member of the House of the Shang. The last king Zhou was a notorious tyrant, who killed even his own uncles for admonishing him. Jizi did not have the heart to leave the kingdom, yet he realized that he could not do anything to enlighten the king. So he feigned insanity. When the dynasty fell, he escaped to another kingdom and hid.

52.	Traditional scholars often take the Outer Trigram, that of Wind, as a symbol of "the eldest daughter" and the Inner Trigram, that of Fire, as a symbol of "the middle daughter". Zhou Zhenfu proposes that Wind is a symbol for "influence" and Fire that of "virtue". He believes that this Hexagram is about the beginning of virtue at home and spreading of influence to others (see Zhou Zhenfu, *Zhouyi yizhu*, p. 131).

53.	I read *sui* 遂 as *zhui* 坠 , meaning "mistakes" (see Xu Zihong, *Zhouyi quanyi*, p. 200).

54.	*Jia* is interpreted as *da* 大, or "large". I adopt Hui Dong's reading of this phrase (see Hui Dong, *Zhouyi shu*, pp. 122-123).

55.	*Gui* 鬼 is literally "ghost". Xu Zihong glosses it as "strangely attired people" (see Xu Zihong, *Zhouyi quanyi, p.* 208).

56.	The translation of this line is based on Lai Zhide's interpretation (see Lai Zhide, *Zhouyi jizhu*, 8:18).

57.	I follow Zhou Zhenfu's reading of this line (see Zhou Zhenfu, *Zhouyi yizhu*, p. 141).

58.	The Trigram consisting of the second, third and fourth lines symbolizes Fire, while the one consisting of the third, fourth and fifth lines symbolizes Water.

59.	Following Wu Xinchu, I read *chuan* 遄 as *duan* 端 (see Wu Xinchu, *Jianming Zhouyi duben*, p. 77).

60.	I punctuate the line in the way as suggested by Hui Dong (see Hui Dong, *Zhouyi shu*, p. 138).

61.	For the meaning of the term *ying shi* 羸 豕 , see Zhou Zhenfu, *Zhouyi yizhu*, p. 156.

62.	Read *bao* 包 as *pao* 疱 (see Wu Xinchu, *Jianming Zhouyi duben*, p. 81).

63.   *Tian* 天 should be interpreted as *tian ran* 天 然 here (see Zhou Zhenfu, *Zhouyi yizhu,* p. 157).

64.   Translation of the phrase based on Wu Xichu, *Jianming Zhouyi duben,* p. 82.

65.   My translation is based on the interpretation of the Ming scholar Lai Zhide, which, ironically, is more relevant to the modern reader than the readings of modern scholars.

66.   I have modified Lai Zhide's reading of the term *qi shan* 岐 山 (for Lai Zhide's original reading, see *Yijing jizhu,* 9:25b-26a)

67.   Lai Zhide glosses *tun* 臀 as "sit" (see Lai Zhide, *Yijing jizhu,* 9:31a).

68.   Hui Dong observes that *yi yue* 劓 刖 should be read as *ni wu* 倪 仉 (see Hui Dong, *Zhouyi shu,* pp. 158 & 160).

69.   Hui Dong points out that the inner trigram, that of *kan,* signifies the *jie gou,* a wood structure with a bucket on one end and a rock on the other (see Hui Dong, *Zhouyi shu,* p. 161). The ancient Chinese used the device to draw water from the well.

70.   Hui Dong glosses *fu* 鮒 as "frogs" (see Hui Dong, *Zhouyi shu,* p. 162). The word 射 , usually pronounced as *she,* is problematic here. I propose to pronounce it as *yu,* as in the phrase *hao er wu yu* 好 尔 无 射 ("I will love you and will never hate you"), where *yu* means "dislike".

71.   I read *ji* 疾   as *ji* 嫉 .

72.   Sha Shaohai suggests that *yi* 亿 is a particle (see Sha Shaohai, *Yigua qianshi,* p. 312).

73.   Wen Yiduo glosses *hungou* 婚 媾   as "friends and relatives" (see Sha Shaohai, *Yigua qianshi,* p. 315).   I adopt his interpretation.

74.   Traditional scholars read *gen* as "to stop/to keep still". Following Sha Shaohai, a number of modern Chinese scholars gloss *gen* as "to look steadily at"

(for Sha Shaohai's reading, see *Yigua qianshi,* p. 317). The lines seem to make better sense if we follow this interpretation.

75.　　　"Flies to" is a free translation for *jian* 渐, which literally means "progressing/advancing gradually".

76.　　　Li Jingchi argues that *xun* 旬 should be read as 姰 or "to live together" (cited in Xu Zihong, *Zhouyi quanyi,* p. 299). Though such a reading makes very good sense for the line, it is not consistent with the general principle of *Changes.* According to the principle, the corresponding line, or the mate, for line 1 is line 4. In this Hexagram, both line 1 and line 4 belong in the *yang* category, and do not make a couple.

77.　　　My translation of this line is based on Xu Zihong's interpretation. For Xu's reading, see *Zhouyi quanyi,* p. 300.

78.　　　For the translation of this line, I opt to follow the punctuation of traditional scholars like Lai Zhide and Hui Dong. Some modern scholars punctuate this line in a different way and their interpretation is quite different from the traditional one (for example, see Sha Shaohai, *Yigua qianshi,* p. 343).

79.　　　I adopt Lai Zhide's reading of *yi* 易 as *yi* 埸 (see Lai Zhide, *Yijing jizhu,* 11:30b).

80.　　　See note 27 above.

81.　　　A number of modern scholars gloss *huan* 涣 as "inundation". But the lines will sound meaningless if one follows this interpretation without inserting a lot of one's own words. The interpretations of traditional scholars like Lai Zhide and Hui Dong are also dubious. I have tried my best to make sense of this obscure Hexagram which, I believe, none of the scholars I have consulted really understand.

82.　　　Zhou Zhenfu observes that the word *jie* 节 (restraint), has been omitted in the phrase *wu jiu* 无 咎 (no regrets). See Zhou Zhenfu, *Zhouyi yizhu,* p. 216.

83.　　　Again, the word *jie* has been omitted before the phrase *hui wang* (see Zhou Zhenfu, *Zhouyi yizhu,* p. 102).

84.   I read *li* 离 as *li* 罹 , "to incur".

85.   Xu Zihong proposes that *lun* 轮 should be read as *lun* 纶 (see Xu Zihong, *Zhouyi quanyi,* p. 341). The translation of this line and the next one is based on Xu's interpretation.

86.   Sha Shaohai quotes Wang Bi and Cheng Yi to argue that *ru* 繻 can be glossed as *ru* 濡 (wet). See Sha Shaohai, *Yigua qianshi,* p. 385.

87.   Gao Heng has suggested that *zhen* may be a personal name (cited in Sha Shaohai, *Yigua qianshi,* p. 390).

Hexagram Chart

Upper Trigram / Lower Trigram	Qian	Zhen	Kan	Gen	Kun	Xun	Li	Dui
Qian	1	34	5	26	11	9	14	43
Zhen	25	51	3	27	24	42	21	17
Kan	6	40	29	4	7	59	64	47
Gen	33	62	39	52	15	53	56	31
Kun	12	16	8	23	2	20	35	45
Xun	44	32	48	18	46	57	50	28
Li	13	55	63	22	36	37	30	49
Dui	10	54	60	41	19	61	38	58

THE BOOK OF CHANGES
《周易》古经

PART ONE
上经

Hexagram 1　　Qian - The Assertive

乾：元亨，利贞。

初九：潜龙，勿用。

九二：见龙在田，利见大人。

九三：君子终日乾乾，夕惕若；厉，无咎。

九四：或跃在渊，无咎。

九五：飞龙在天，利见大人。

上九：亢龙，有悔。

用九：见群龙无首，吉。

Hexagram 2　　Kun - Inner Strength

坤：元亨，利牝马之贞。君子有攸往，先迷后得主，利；
　　　西南得朋，东北丧朋，安贞吉。

初六：履霜，坚冰至。

六二：直方大，不习无不利。

六三：含章，可贞。或从王事，无成，有终。

六四：括囊，无咎无誉。

六五：黄裳，元吉。

上六：龙战于野，其血玄黄。

用六：利永贞。

Hexagram 3   Tun - Difficulty

屯：元亨，利贞。勿用有悠往，利建侯。

初九：磐桓，利居贞，利建侯。

六二：屯如，邅如，乘马班如。匪寇，婚媾，女子贞不字，十
　　　年乃字。

六三：即鹿无虞，唯入于林中。君子几，不如舍，往吝。

六四：乘马班如，求婚媾，往，吉无不利。

九五：屯其膏，小贞吉，大贞凶。

上六：乘马班如，泣血涟如。

Hexagram 4   Meng - Wild Grass, the Undisciplined

蒙：亨。匪我求童蒙，童蒙求我。初筮告，再三渎，渎
　　　则不告。利贞。

初六：发蒙，利用刑人，用说桎梏以往，吝。

九二：包蒙吉，纳妇吉，子克家。

六三：勿用取女，见金夫，不有躬，无攸利。

六四：困蒙，吝。

六五：童蒙，吉。

上九：击蒙。不利为寇，利御寇。

Hexagram 5   Xu - Waiting

需：有孚，光亨，贞吉。利涉大川。

初九：需于郊，利用恒，无咎。

九二：需于沙，小有言，终吉。

九三：需于泥，致寇至。

六四：需于血，出自穴。

九五：需于酒食，贞吉。

上六：入于穴，有不速之客三人来。敬之，终吉。

Hexagram 6　Song - Litigation

䷅讼：有孚，窒惕。中吉，终凶。利见大人，不利涉大川。

初六：不永所事，小有言，终吉。

九二：不克讼，归而逋其邑人三百户，无眚。

六三：食旧德，贞厉，终吉。或从王事，无成。

九四：不克讼，复即命渝，安贞吉。

九五：讼，元吉。

上九：或锡之鞶带，终朝三褫之。

Hexagram 7　Shi - The Army

䷆师：贞丈人吉，无咎。

初六：师出以律，否臧，凶。

九二：在师中，吉，无咎。王三锡命。

六三：师或舆尸，凶。

六四：师左次，无咎。

六五：田有禽，利执言，无咎。长子帅师，弟子舆尸，贞凶。

上六：大君有命，开国承家，小人勿用。

Hexagram 8   Bi - Alliance

比：吉，原筮元，永贞无咎。不宁方来，后夫凶。

初六：有孚，比之，无咎。有孚，盈缶，终来有它，吉。

六二：比之自内，贞吉。

六三：比之匪人。

六四：外比之，贞吉。

九五：显比，王用三驱，失前禽。邑人不诫，吉。

上六：比之无首，凶。

Hexagram 9   Xiao Xu - Building Up Influence

小畜：亨。密云不雨，自我西郊。

初九：复自道，何其咎？吉。

九二：牵复，吉。

九三：舆说辐，夫妻反目。

六四：有孚，血去，惕出，无咎。

九五：有孚，挛如，富以其邻。

上九：既雨既处，尚德载，妇贞厉。月几望，君子征，凶。

Hexagram 10 Lü - Following

履虎尾，不咥人，亨。

初九：素履往，无咎。

九二：履道坦坦，幽人贞吉。

六三：眇能视，跛能履，履虎尾，咥人，凶。武人为于大君。

九四：履虎尾，愬愬，终吉。

九五：夬履，贞厉。

上九：视履，考祥其旋，元吉。

Hexagram 11 Tai - Smooth Interaction

䷊ 泰：小往大来，吉，亨。

初九：拔茅，茹以其汇，征吉。

九二：包荒，用冯河。不遐遗，朋亡，得尚于中行。

九三：无平不陂，无往不复。艰贞，无咎。勿恤其孚，于食
有福。

六四：翩翩，不富以其邻，不戒以孚。

六五：帝乙归妹，以祉元吉。

上六：城复于隍，勿用师，自邑告命，贞吝。

Hexagram 12 Pi - Obstruction

䷋ 否之匪人，不利君子贞，大往小来。

初六：拔茅，茹以其汇，贞吉，亨。

六二：包承，小人吉，大人否，亨。

六三：包羞。

九四：有命无咎。畴离祉。

九五：休否，大人吉。其亡其亡，系于苞桑。

上九：倾否，先否后喜。

Hexagram 13   Tong Ren - Joining Forces

同人于野，亨。利涉大川，利君子贞。

初九：同人于门，无咎。
六二：同人于宗，吝。
九三：伏戎于莽，升其高陵，三岁不兴。
九四：乘其墉，弗克攻，吉。
九五：同人，先号咷而后笑，大师克相遇。
上九：同人于郊，无悔。

Hexagram 14   Da You - Great Wealth

大有：元亨。

初九：无交害。匪咎，艰则无咎。
九二：大车以载，有攸往，无咎。
九三：公用亨于天子，小人弗克。
九四：匪其彭，无咎。
六五：厥孚交如威如，吉。
上九：自天祐之，吉无不利。

Hexagram 15   Qian - Modesty

谦：亨，君子有终。

初六：谦谦君子，用涉大川，吉。
六二：鸣谦，贞吉。

九三：劳谦，君子有终，吉。

六四：无不利，㧑谦。

六五：不富以其邻，利用侵伐，无不利。

上六：鸣谦，利用行师，征邑国。

Hexagram 16 Yu - The Joyous

豫：利建侯，行师。

初六：鸣豫，凶。

六二：介于石，不终日，贞吉。

六三：盱豫悔，迟有悔。

九四：由豫，大有得，勿疑朋盍簪。

六五：贞疾，恒不死。

上六：冥豫成；有渝，无咎。

Hexagram 17 Sui - Alignment

随：元亨，利贞，无咎。

初九：官有渝，贞吉，出门交有功。

六二：系小子，失丈夫。

六三：系丈夫，失小子。随有求得，利居贞。

九四：随有获，贞凶。有孚在道，以明，何咎。

九五：孚于嘉，吉。

上六：拘系之，乃从维之，王用亨于西山。

Hexagram 18   Gu - [The Parents] Enterprise

䷑蛊：元亨，利涉大川。先甲三日，后甲三日。

初六：干父之蛊，有子考，无咎。厉，终吉。

九二：干母之蛊，不可贞。

九三：干父之蛊，小有悔，无大咎。

六四：裕父之蛊，往见，吝。

六五：干父之蛊，用誉。

上九：不事王候，高尚其事。

Hexagram 19   Lin - Approaches to Ruling

䷒临：元亨，利贞。至于八月有凶。

初九：咸临，贞吉。

九二：咸临，吉，无不利。

六三：甘临，无攸利。既忧之，无咎。

六四：至临，无咎。

六五：知临，大君之宜，吉。

上六：敦临，吉，无咎。

Hexagram 20   Guan - Observation

䷓观：盥而不荐，有孚颙若。

初六：童观，小人无咎，君子吝。

六二：阚观，利女贞。

六三：观我生，进退。

六四：观国之光，利用宾于王。

九五：观我生，君子无咎。

上九：观其生，君子无咎。

Hexagram 21　Shi Ke - Biting / Law Enforcement

噬嗑：亨，利用狱。

初九：屦校灭趾，无咎。

六二：噬肤灭鼻，无咎。

六三：噬腊肉，遇毒，小吝，无咎。

九四：噬乾胏，得金矢，利艰贞，吉。

六五：噬乾肉，得黄金，贞厉，无咎。

上九：何校灭耳，凶。

Hexagram 22　Bi - Adornment

贲：亨，小利有攸往。

初九：贲其趾，舍车而徒。

六二：贲其须。

九三：贲如，濡如，永贞吉。

六四：贲如，皤如，白马翰如，匪寇，婚媾。

六五：贲于丘园，束帛戋戋，吝，终吉。

上九：白贲，无咎。

Hexagram 23　Bo - Falling Apart

剥：不利有攸往。

初六：剥床以足，蔑，贞凶。

六二：剥床以辨，蔑，贞凶。

六三：剥之，无咎。

六四：剥床以肤，凶。

六五：贯鱼以宫人宠，无不利。

上九：硕果不食，君子得舆，小人剥庐。

Hexagram 24 Fu - Returning

复：亨，出入无疾，朋来无咎。反复其道，七日来复，
利有攸往。

初九：不远复，无祇悔，元吉。

六二：休复，吉。

六三：频复，厉，无咎。

六四：中行独复。

六五：敦复，无悔。

上六：迷复，凶，有灾眚。用行师，终有大败，以其国君，
凶，至于十年不克征。

Hexagram 25 Wu Wang - The Unexpected

无妄：元亨利贞。其匪正，有眚，不利有攸往。

初九：无妄，往吉。

六二：不耕获，不菑畲，则利有攸往。

六三：无妄之灾，或系之牛，行人之得，邑人之灾。

九四：可贞，无咎。

九五：无妄之疾，勿药有喜。

上九：无妄，行有眚，无攸利。

Hexagram 26　Da Xu - Building Up Great Strength

大畜：利贞。不家食，吉，利涉大川。

初九：有厉，利已。

九二：舆说輹。

九三：良马逐，利艰贞，日闲舆卫，利有攸往。

六四：童牛之牿，元吉。

六五：豮豕之牙，吉。

上九：何天之衢，亨。

Hexagram 27　Yi - Mouth / Providing Nourishment

颐：贞吉。观颐，自求口实。

初九：舍尔灵龟，观我朵颐，凶。

六二：颠颐，拂经于丘颐，征凶。

六三：拂颐，贞凶，十年勿用，无攸利。

六四：颠颐，吉。虎视眈眈，其欲逐逐，无咎。

六五：拂经，居贞吉。不可涉大川。

上九：由颐，厉，吉。利涉大川。

Hexagram 28　Da Guo - Excess

大过：栋桡，利有攸往，亨。

初六：藉用白茅，无咎。

九二：枯杨生稊，老夫得其女妻，无不利。

九三：栋桡，凶。

九四：栋隆，吉。有它，吝。

九五：枯杨生华，老妇得其士夫，无咎，无誉。

上六：过涉灭顶，凶，无咎。

Hexagram 29 Kan - Abyss

坎：有孚维心，亨，行有尚。

初六：习坎，入于坎窞，凶。

九二：坎有险，求小来。

六三：来之坎，坎险且枕。入于坎窞，勿用。

六四：樽酒，簋贰，用缶，纳约自牖，终无咎。

九五：坎不盈，祇既平，无咎。

上六：糸用徽纆，寘于丛棘，三岁不得，凶。

Hexagram 30 Li - Fire / Fiery Temper

离：利贞，亨。畜牝牛，吉。

初九：履错然，敬之，无咎。

六二：黄离，元吉。

九三：日昃之离，不鼓缶而歌，则大耋之嗟。凶。

九四：突如，其来如，焚如，死如，弃如。

六五：出涕沱若，戚嗟若，吉。

上九：王用出征，有嘉折首，获匪其丑，无咎。

PART TWO
下经
Hexagram 31　Xian - Move / Influence

咸：亨，利贞。取女吉。

初六：咸其拇。

六二：咸其腓，凶。居吉。

九三：咸其股，执其随，往吝。

九四：贞吉，悔亡。憧憧往来，朋从尔思。

九五：咸其脢，无悔。

上六：咸其辅颊舌。

Hexagram 32　Heng - Constancy

恒：亨，无咎。利贞，利有攸往。

初六：浚恒，贞凶，无攸利。

九二：悔亡。

九三：不恒其德，或承之羞，贞吝。

九四：田无禽。

六五：恒其德，贞妇人吉，夫子凶。

上六：振恒，凶。

Hexagram 33　Dun - Retreat

遁：亨，小利贞。

初六：遁尾，厉，勿用有攸往。

六二：执之用黄牛之革，莫之胜说。

九三：糸遁，有疾厉；畜臣妾，吉。

九四：好遁，君子吉，小人否。

九五：嘉遁，贞吉。

上九：肥遁，无不利。

Hexagram 34 Da Zhuang - Great Strength

大壮：利贞。

初九：壮于趾，征凶，有孚。

九二：贞吉。

九三：小人用壮，君子用罔，贞厉。羝羊触藩，羸其角。

九四：贞吉，悔亡。藩决不羸，壮于大舆之輹。

六五：丧羊于易，无悔。

上六：羝羊触藩，不能退，不能遂，无攸利，艰则吉。

Hexagram 35 Jin - Advancement

晋：康侯，用锡马蕃庶，昼日三接。

初六：晋如，摧如，贞吉。罔孚裕，无咎。

六二：晋如，愁如，贞吉。受兹介福于其王母。

六三：众允，悔亡。

九四：晋如，鼫鼠，贞厉。

六五：悔亡，失得勿恤，往吉，无不利。

上九：晋其角，维。用伐邑，厉，吉，无咎。贞吝。

234

Hexagram 36 Ming Yi - Darkening of the Light

䷣明夷：利艰贞。

初九：明夷于飞，垂其翼；君子于行，三日不食。有攸往，
　　　主人有言。

六二：明夷，夷于左股，用拯马壮，吉。

九三：明夷于南狩，得其大首，不可疾，贞。

六四：入于左腹，获明夷之心，于出门庭。

六五：箕子之明夷，利贞。

上六：不明，晦，初登于天，后入于地。

Hexagram 37 Jia Ren - The Family

䷤家人：利女贞。

初九：闲有家，悔亡。

六二：无攸遂，在中馈，贞吉。

九三：家人嗃嗃，悔厉，吉。妇子嘻嘻，终吝。

六四：富家大吉。

九五：王假有家，勿恤，吉。

上九：有孚，威如，终吉。

Hexagram 38 Kui - Parting

䷥睽：小事吉。

初九：悔亡，丧马，勿逐，自复；见恶人，无咎。

九二：遇主于巷，无咎。

六三：见舆曳，其牛掣，其人天且劓。无初有终。

九四：睽孤，遇元夫，交孚，厉，无咎。

六五：悔亡，厥宗噬肤，往何咎。

上九：睽孤，见豕负涂，载鬼一车。先张之弧，后说之弧，匪寇，婚媾。往遇雨则吉。

Hexagram 39　Jian - Obstacles

蹇：利西南，不利东北。利见大人，贞吉。

初六：往蹇，来誉。

六二：王臣蹇蹇，匪躬之故。

九三：往蹇，来反。

六四：往蹇，来连。

九五：大蹇，朋来。

上六：往蹇，来硕，吉，利见大人。

Hexagram 40　Jie - Removing Obstacles

解：利西南。无所往，其来复，吉。有攸往，夙吉。

初六：无咎。

九二：田获三狐，得黄矢、贞吉。

六三：负且乘，致寇至，贞吝。

九四：解而拇，朋至，斯孚。

六五：君子维有解，吉。有孚于小人。

上六：公用射隼于高墉之上，获之，无不利。

Hexagram 41   Sun - Cutting Down

损：有孚，元吉，无咎，可贞，利有攸往。曷之用？二
　　簋可用享。

初九：巳事遄往，无咎；酌损之。

九二：利贞，征凶，弗损，益之。

六三：三人行则损一人，一人行则得其友。

六四：损其疾，使遄，有喜，无咎。

六五：或益之十朋之龟，弗克违，元吉。

上九：弗损，益之，无咎，贞吉，利有攸往。得臣无家。

Hexagram 42   Yi - Increase

益：利有攸往，利涉大川。

初九：利用为大作，元吉，无咎。

六二：或益之十朋以龟，弗克违，永贞吉。王用享于帝，吉。

六三：益之用凶事，无咎。有孚，中行，告公用圭。

六四：中行告公，从，利用为依迁国。

九五：有孚，惠心，勿问，元吉，有孚，惠我德。

上九：莫益之，或击之，立心勿恒，凶。

Hexagram 43   Guai - The Decisive

夬：扬于王庭，孚号有厉。告自邑，不利即戎，利有攸
　　往。

初九：壮于前趾，往不胜，为咎。

九二：惕号，莫夜有戎，勿恤。

九三：壮于頄，有凶。君子夬夬，独行，遇雨，若濡，有愠，无咎。

九四：臀无肤，其行次且。牵羊，悔亡，闻言不信。

九五：苋陆夬夬中行，无咎。

上六：无号，终有凶。

Hexagram 44 Gou - Encountering

姤：女壮，勿用取女。

初六：糸于金柅，贞吉。有攸往，见凶。羸豕孚蹢躅。

九二：包有鱼，无咎。不利宾。

九三：臀无肤，其行次且，厉，无大咎。

九四：包无鱼，起凶。

九五：以杞包瓜，含章，有陨自天。

上九：姤其角，吝；无咎。

Hexagram 45 Cui - Gathering Together

萃：亨，王假有庙，利见大人，亨，利贞。用大牲吉，利有攸往。

初六：有孚，不终，乃乱乃萃。若号，一握为笑。勿恤，往无咎。

六二：引吉，无咎，孚，乃利用禴。

六三：萃如嗟如。无攸利。往无咎，小吝。

九四：大吉，无咎。

九五：萃有位，无咎。匪孚，元永贞，悔亡。
上六：赍咨涕洟，无咎。

Hexagram 46 Sheng - Ascending

升：元亨，用见大人，勿恤。南征吉。

初六：允升，大吉。
九二：孚，乃利用禴，无咎。
九三：升虚邑。
六四：王用亨于岐山，吉，无咎。
六五：贞吉，升阶。
上六：冥升，利于不息之贞。

Hexagram 47 Kun - In Plight

困：亨，贞大人吉，无咎。有言不信。

初六：臀困于株木，入于幽谷，三岁不觌。
九二：困于酒食，朱绂方来，利用享祀。征凶。
六三：困于石，据于蒺藜。入于其宫，不见其妻，凶。
九四：来徐徐，困于金车，吝，有终。
九五：劓刖，困于赤绂。乃徐有说，利用祭祀。
上六：困于葛藟，于臲卼，曰动悔有悔，征吉。

Hexagram 48 Jing - The Well

井：改邑不改井，无丧无得。往来井井，汔至，亦未繘
　　井，羸其瓶，凶。

初六：井泥不食，旧井无禽。

九二：井谷射鲋，瓮敝漏。

九三：井渫不食，为我心恻，可用汲，王明，并受其福。

六四：井甃，无咎。

九五：井洌，寒泉，食。

上六：井收勿幕，有孚，元吉。

Hexagram 49 Ge - Reform

革：巳日乃孚。元亨，利贞，悔亡。

初九：巩用黄牛之革。

六二：巳日乃革之，征吉，无咎。

九三：征凶，贞厉。革言三就，有孚。

九四：悔亡。有孚，改命，吉。

九五：大人虎变，未占有孚。

上六：君子豹变，小人革面，征凶。居贞吉。

Hexagram 50 Ding - The Tripod / Renewal

鼎：元吉，亨。

初六：鼎颠趾，利出否，得妾以其子，无咎。

九二：鼎有实，我仇有疾，不我能即，吉。

九三：鼎耳革，其行塞，雉膏不食，方雨亏悔，终吉。

九四：鼎折足，覆公餗，其形渥。凶。

六五：鼎黄耳，金铉，利贞。

上九：鼎玉铉，大吉，无不利。

Hexagram 51 Zhen - Thunder / Shock

震：亨，震来虩虩，笑言哑哑，震惊百里，不丧匕鬯。

初九：震来虩虩，后笑言哑哑，吉。

六二：震来历，亿丧贝。跻于九陵，勿逐，七日得。

六三：震苏苏，震行无眚。

九四：震遂泥。

六五：震往来历，意无丧，有事。

上六：震索索，视矍矍，征凶。震不于其躬，于其邻，无咎。
婚媾有言。

Hexagram 52 Gen - Mountain / Steadiness

艮：艮其背，不获其身，行其庭，不见其人，无咎。

初六：艮其趾，无咎，利永贞。

六二：艮其腓，不拯其随，其心不快。

九三：艮其限，列其夤，厉，薰心。

六四：艮其身，无咎。

六五：艮其辅，言有序，悔亡。

上九：敦艮，吉。

Hexagram 53 Jian - Gradual Progress

渐：女归，吉，利贞。

初六：鸿渐于干，小子厉，有言，无咎。

六二：鸿渐于磐，饮食衎衎，吉。

241

九三：鸿渐于陆，夫征不复，妇孕不育，凶。利御寇。

六四：鸿渐于木，或得其桷，无咎。

九五：鸿渐于陵，妇三岁不孕，终莫之胜，吉。

上九：鸿渐于陆，其羽可用为仪，吉。

Hexagram 54 Gui Mei - Marrying a Daughter Off

䷵归妹：征凶，无攸利。

初九：归妹以娣，跛能履，征吉。

九二：眇能视，利幽人之贞。

六三：归妹以须，反归以娣。

九四：归妹愆期，迟归有时。

六五：帝乙归妹，其君之袂不如其娣之袂良。月几望，吉。

上六：女承筐无实，士刲羊无血。无攸利。

Hexagram 55　Feng - Enlargement / Expansion

䷶丰：亨，王假之，勿忧，宜日中。

初九：遇其配主，虽旬无咎，往有尚。

六二：丰其蔀，日中见斗。往得疑疾，有孚，发若。吉。

九三：丰其沛，日中见沫，折其右肱，无咎。

九四：丰其蔀，日中见斗，遇其夷主，吉。

六五：来章，有庆誉，吉。

上六：丰其屋，蔀其家，阒其户，阒其无人，三岁不觌，凶。

Hexagram 56 Lü - Travelling

旅：小亨，旅，贞吉。

初六：旅琐琐，斯其所取灾。

六二：旅即次，怀其资，得童仆，贞〔吉〕。

九三：旅焚其次，丧其童仆，贞厉。

九四：旅于处，得其资斧，我心不快。

六五：射雉，一矢亡，终以誉命。

上九：鸟焚其巢，旅人先笑后号咷，丧牛于易，凶。

Hexagram 57 Xun - The Yielding

巽：小亨，利有攸往，利见大人。

初六：进退，利武人之贞。

九二：巽在床下，用史巫，纷若，吉，无咎。

九三：频巽，吝。

六四：悔亡，田获三品。

九五：贞吉、悔亡，无不利，无初有终。先庚三日，后庚三
日，吉。

上九：巽在床下，丧其资斧，贞凶。

Hexagram 58 Dui - Swamp / The Pleasing

兑：亨，利贞。

初九：和兑，吉。

九二：孚兑，吉。悔亡。

六三：来兑，凶。

九四：商兑未宁，介疾，有喜。

九五：孚于剥，有厉。

上六：引兑。

Hexagram 59　Huan - Breaking Away

涣：亨，王假有庙，利涉大川，利贞。

初六：用拯马壮，吉。

九二：涣奔其机，悔亡。

六三：涣其躬，无悔。

六四：涣其群，元吉。涣有丘，匪夷所思。

九五：涣，汗其大号，涣，王居无咎。

上九：涣其血，去，逖出，无咎。

Hexagram 60　Jie - Self-Restraint

节：亨。苦节不可贞。

初九：不出户庭，无咎。

九二：不出户庭，凶。

六三：不节若，则嗟若，无咎。

六四：安节，亨。

九五：甘节，吉，往有尚。

上六：苦节，贞凶，悔亡。

Hexagram 61　Zhong Fu - Sincerity / Faithfulness

中孚：豚鱼吉，利涉大川。利贞 。

初九：虞吉，有它不燕。

九二：鸣鹤在阴，其子和之。我有好爵，吾与尔靡之。

六三：得敌，或鼓或罢，或泣或歌。

六四：月几望，马匹亡，无咎。

九五：有孚挛如，无咎。

上九：翰音登于天，贞凶。

Hexagram 62　Xiao Guo - Minor Mistakes

小过：亨，利贞。可小事，不可大事。飞鸟遗之音，不
　　　宜上，宜下。大吉。

初六：飞鸟以凶。

六二：过其祖，遇其妣，不及其君，遇其臣，无咎。

九三：费过防之，从或戕之，凶。

九四：无咎，弗过遇之，往厉必戒，勿用，永贞。

六五：密云不雨，自我西郊，公弋取彼在穴。

上六：弗遇过之，飞鸟离之，凶，是谓灾眚。

Hexagram 63　Ji Ji - After Crossing / Mission Accomplished

既济：亨，小利贞。初吉，终乱。

初九：曳其轮，濡其尾，无咎。

六二：妇丧其茀，勿逐，七日得。

九三：高宗伐鬼方，三年克之，小人勿用。

六四：繻有衣袽，终日戒。

九五：东邻杀牛，不如西邻之禴祭，实受其福。

上六：濡其首，厉。

Hexagram 64　Wei Ji - Before Crossing / Mission To Be Accomplished

未济：亨。小狐汔济，濡其尾，无攸利。

初六：濡其尾，吝。

九二：曳其轮，贞吉。

六三：未济，征凶，利涉大川。

九四：贞吉，悔亡。震用伐鬼方，三年有赏于大国。

六五：贞吉，无悔，君子之光，有孚吉。

上九：有孚于饮酒，无咎。濡其首，有孚失是。

Other Asiapac Titles:
Chinese Art of Divination

THE I CHING

The I Ching is one of the oldest classics in the world and is widely regarded as a storehouse of wisdom for guidance in the conduct of life. This comic edition is designed for practical use and seeks to unravel the mystery of The I Ching by exploring the origins and explaining the applications of the ancient art of divination.

FENG SHUI KIT:
The Chinese Way to Health, Wealth and Happiness, at Home and at Work

The *book* contains full instructions and draws upon the wisdom of Man-Ho Kwok, one of the few fully qualified feng shui masters living in Europe. Use the *feng shui compass* to discover quickly and easily the best position for everything. And discover how to place the *pa kua mirror* provided to deflect any malign forces and spirits.

Asiapac Collectors' Series

ANTIQUE CERAMICS
Durable and beautiful, antique ceramics have a timeless appeal. As good pieces become harder to find, being able to differentiate the genuine from the fakes becomes crucial to the collectors. Written by well-known art critic Lee Ying Ho, the book gives an understanding of the origins and types of porcelain. Readers will also be advised on how to identify porcelain by motifs, marks and other characteristics to enjoy its beauty as well as make a wise investment.

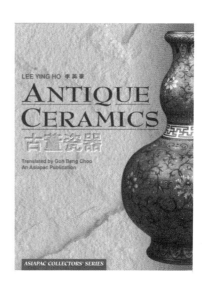

JADEITE
The overwhelming fascination with the gemstone has led to the creation of many beautiful pieces of jadeite jewellery which, with the passage of time, have enjoyed an increase in value and been eagerly traded at auctions.

In this volume, Lee Ying Ho shares with readers the origin, appreciation and worth of jadeite, together with the maintenance of jadeite jewellery, the identification of fakes rampant on the market, and the methods of their production.